G000244970

*QOCS AND A QUALITY PRODUCT*

*The reason Kerry is listened to on costs and proc⟨⟩ detailed knowledge of the rules coupled with (m⟨⟩ experience as a practising solicitor and senior partner. Here the detailed knowledge and experience are combined in a thorough and readable text. QOCS are a part of life for litigators. Detailed knowledge of the rules, and vagaries, of QOCS is now a necessity for all litigators. This is, without a doubt, essential reading.*

Gordon Exall, Barrister, Hardwicke Chambers

**Unlike the Rules, this book has been admirably thought through and I will be delving into it repeatedly.**

Ian Foster, Law Costs Draftsman

*This is the QOCS Bible.*

Sofia Ashraf, Barrister

**Very knowledgeable and entertaining to boot.**

Anthony McCarthy, Macks Solicitors

*When one wishes to find a decent curry in say Basingstoke, one Googles "curryhouseBasingstoke". When one has a legal problem, particularly personal injury or Jackson related, one Googles "KerryUnderwood". It really is that simple! There is just no need to look elsewhere.*

Andrew Twambley, CEO, InjuryLawyers4U

I

Extracts from Gordon Exall's review on civillitigationbrief.wordpress.com.

*Kerry clearly wants you to read the book all the way through, like a Grisham novel, only, of course, much more gripping...*

*Practical and hard headed guidance...*

*With all the pressures on the modern lawyer it is often forgotten that we are in the knowledge business. Here we have knowledge aplenty. Knowledge that is combined with clear and pragmatic guidance. Buying this is not wasted money, reading it is not wasted time.*

*Many law books are over-priced. This is not. The only mystery is what, precisely, the white cliffs are supposed to represent...*

An email from the author explaining the last point.

*Those are not white cliffs. It is an ice shelf off of Antarctica. Since I took the picture it has fallen in to the sea (the ice shelf not the picture). So it could be that Jackson is the global warming of the law, or that, as with icebergs 90% is below the surface, or the contrast between dark and light. I just like the picture!*

# Qualified One-Way Costs Shifting, Section 57 and Set-Off

*Kerry Underwood*

Partner, Underwoods Solicitors

To

My Goddaughter

# Phoebe

Law Abroad PLC

First softback edition printed 2016 in the United Kingdom.

A catalogue record for this book is available from the British Library.

ISBN 978-0-9935349-0-4

Published by Law Abroad Publishing, part of Law Abroad PLC

For more copies of this book, please email: d.barnard@lawabroad.net

Tel: 01442 430900

Designed and set by Law Abroad Publishing, part of Law Abroad PLC, 79 Marlowes, Hemel Hempstead, Hertfordshire, HP1 1LF

http://www.underwoods-solicitors.co.uk/

Printed in Great Britain by Halstan & Co Ltd, 2-10 Plantation Road, Amersham, Buckinghamshire, HP6 6HJ

# THANK YOU!

**Special thanks to**:

Doné Barnard
Jamiel Zaman

**Thanks to:**

British International School of Stavanger, Norway
Cynthia Barnes
His Honour Michael Cook
Gordon Exall
Malcolm George
Mark Harvey
PJ Kirby QC
Claire Long
Robert Males
Anna Patsalides
Mike Penning MP
Phoebe Ranger
Professor Dominic Regan
Rachel Rothwell
Stuart Thompson
Lauren Turner
Andrew Twambley
Nikki Valentine
Leah Waller
My Blog Subscribers
My followers on Twitter

**I am particularly grateful to Professor Dominic Regan for proof reading this book. Any remaining mistakes are mine.**

## The Author

Kerry Underwood is a solicitor and is senior partner of Underwoods Solicitors. He is a lecturer, writer, broadcaster and former Employment Judge.

Kerry writes and edits the Costs and Funding section of Butterworths Personal Injury Litigation Service and is a regular contributor to Litigation Funding, New Law Journal, Solicitors Journal, Claims Magazine and the Law Society's Civil Justice Section Newsletter.

He pioneered Conditional Fee Agreements, TV advertising by lawyers and off-shoring work to South Africa.

Former Councillor and Parliamentary Candidate.

Kerry travels extensively and home is his beloved adopted town of Hemel Hempstead. Underwoods Solicitors sponsor Hemel Hempstead Town Football Club and Hemel Stags Rugby League Club.

Interests include football, cricket, gardening and reading. Kerry still plays cricket and is Chairman of his village club Bovingdon Cricket Club.

Nelson Mandela, TS Eliot and Elvis are amongst his heroes.

Kerry supports Queens Park Rangers.

See Kerry's blog at: kerryunderwood.wordpress.com

## Other titles by Kerry Underwood

Small Claims, Fixed Costs and Portals
Wasted Costs and Third Party Costs
Litigants in Person
Court and Tribunal Fees and Remissions
Conditional Fee Agreements, Damages-Based Agreements and Contingency Fees
Selected Writings Volume 1
Selected Writings Volume 2

## Non – Law books

My Dad and Other Pieces

**What are the roots that clutch, what branches grow
Out of this stony rubbish?**

The Burial of the Dead
The Waste Land
T.S. Eliot

**"Without lawyers, judges and courts, there is no access to justice and therefore no rule of law, and without the rule of law, society collapses"**

Lord Neuberger
Supreme Court President
10 April 2015

**USEFUL BLOGS AND WEBSITES**

1.  Kerry Underwood – https://kerryunderwood.wordpress.com/

2.  Civil Litigation Brief, Gordon Exall -
    https://civillitigationbrief.wordpress.com/

3.  Legal Costs Blog, Simon Gibbs - http://www.gwslaw.co.uk/blog/

4.  Sarah Robson -
    http://www.sarahrobsonbarrister.co.uk/default.html

5.  Professor Dominic Regan -
    http://profdominicregan.blogspot.co.uk/

6.  Parliament - http://services.parliament.uk/bills/

7.  The Supreme Court - https://www.supremecourt.uk/

8.  High Court - https://www.judiciary.gov.uk/you-and-the-
    judiciary/going-to-court/high-court/

9.  Court of Appeal - https://www.justice.gov.uk/courts/rcj-rolls-
    building/court-of-appeal

10. Bailli - http://www.bailii.org/

11. Legislation - http://www.legislation.gov.uk/

## HOW TO USE THIS BOOK

Readers will obtain far greater value out of this book by referring to the post on my blog: Kerry on QOCS: Book Update and Links, where every statute, statutory instrument, case, civil procedure rule and practice direction etc. can be accessed in full.

My blog can be seen at:kerryunderwood.wordpress.com.

You can subscribe to my blog by visiting the address above and scrolling down to the bottom of the archive posts list on the right hand side of the page where it says email subscription.

Type your email address and click subscribe; once you receive the email click the link in the email and you have subscribed.

All of the references appear in Part VI of this book, starting at page 217. Simply go to the case or whatever on the blog, click on the link and it will open.

Thus the full text of the entire statute law, case law, civil procedure rules, Practice Directions and other publications can be accessed in seconds through the blog.

It also gives links to all my other blog posts. For example the interplay between QOCS and Part 36 is crucial. I deal with that in this book but my blog post – Part 36: The Dry Salvages – goes into far greater detail about all matters relating to Part 36.

I also constantly update this book, chapter by chapter, on the blog.

The blog has at the end a comments section. Please leave comments, ask questions and let me know of any cases etc that you are involved in.

Thank you.

Kerry Underwood

March 2016

x

# PARTS AND CHAPTERS

**Part I – WHAT IS COVERED?**

1. Introduction

2. Scope

3. Section 57

4. Structure of CPR 44.12 to 44.17

**Part II - EXCEPTIONS**

5. Fundamental Dishonesty

6. Pre – Jackson Funding Agreements

7. Part 36

8. Discontinuance, Strike – out and Summary Judgment

9.  Financial Benefit of Another

10. Miscellaneous

**Part III - STATUTES ETC**

11. Statutes etc.

**Part IV - EXTENDING QUALIFIED ONE-WAY COSTS SHIFTING**

12.  Extending Qualified One-Way Costs Shifting

**Part V - SET – OFF**

13. Set-Off

**Part VI – REFERENCES**

14. References

# CONTENTS

**Part I – WHAT IS COVERED**

**1. INTRODUCTION**   3

     History   3

     Modern Times   5

     Interplay with Section 57 Criminal Justice and Courts Act 2015   6

     Structure of the Book   8

     Summary   9

     Exercise   11

**2. SCOPE**   14

     Type of Work   14

     Issued Proceedings In England & Wales   15

     Place of Injury   16

     Date of Injury   16

     Pre – Action Disclosure   17

     Hybrid Claims   17

     Section 57   19

     Small Claims – Section 57   20

     QOCS   21

Appeals 22

Section 57 22

QOCS 23

Liability Appeals 24

Quantum Appeals 24

Defendants' Appeals 25

Multi-Party Claims 26

Legally - Aided Claims 27

Motor Insurers Bureau Claims 28

Uninsured Drivers 28

Untraced Drivers 28

Qualified One Way Costs Shifting 30

Appeals 31

Summary 32

Criminal Injuries Compensation Authority
(CICA) Claims 33

Discrimination Cases 36

Actual Injury 36

Employment Tribunals and QOCS 37

Employment Tribunals and Section 57 37

Injury to Feelings 38

Shorter Oxford English Dictionary                    38

Impairment                                           38

Impair                                               38

Impaired                                          38, 39

Roget's Thesaurus: Impair                            39

Roget's Thesaurus: Impaired                          39

Roget's Thesaurus Impairment                         39

Summary                                              45

QOCS                                                 45

Section 57                                           45

Children's Cases                                     46

Those Lacking Capacity                               46

Costs Proceedings                                    46

Simmons v Castle 10% uplift                          48

3.  **SECTION 57**                                   53

Commencement                                         53

Effect                                               54

Related Claim                                        55

Substantial injustice                                55

Costs                                                           56

Definitions                                                     56

Criminal Proceedings                                            58

Problem areas                                                   59

Risk assessment                                                 59

Success Fee and Charge to Client                               60

After-the-Event Insurance                                      61

Self-insurance                                                  62

Client Care Letter Wording                                     62

Substantial Injustice                                          64

Level of Burden of Proof re Substantial Injustice             66

What might be covered?                                         67

Children's cases                                               68

Claimants lacking capacity                                     69

Loss of huge award                                            69

Other matters                                                 69

Cost to state                                                 69

Fundamental Dishonesty and Costs Proceedings                  70

Section 57 and Part 36                                        71

Section 57 and Proportionate Costs Orders                     72

Case Law                                                          73

The Irish Experience                                             74

Criminal Liability                                              82

Criminal Justice and Courts Act 2015                            83

Civil Liability and Courts Act 2004                             85

4.   THE STRUCTURE OF CPR 44.12 to 44.17                        88

Restriction is on enforcement, not the order                    88

Partial enforcement without leave                               89

Full enforcement without leave                                  90

Full enforcement with leave                                     90

Ambiguities                                                     90

Set-off under CPR                                               93

Interim payments and CRU                                        94

Part II - EXCEPTIONS

5.   FUNDAMENTAL DISHONESTY                                      97

Claimant Wins                                                   99

Claimant Loses                                                  99

Summers v Fairclough Homes Ltd [2012] UKSC 26                  105

Other cases                                                    109

Alpha Rocks Solicitors v Alade [2015] EWCA Civ 685             111

The Defence View                                          113

Procedure under QOCS re Fundamental Dishonesty           113

Advice re Fundamental Dishonesty                          115

Multi-party cases                                         116

6.  **PRE - JACKSON FUNDING AGREEMENTS**                  117

Pre-Action Disclosure                                    118

Pre 1 April 2013 Conditional Fee Agreements,
ATE etc                                                   118

Nil Success Fee                                           120

Appeals where recoverable additional liability in
relation to original hearing                             124

Joining new parties post 1 April 2013                    125

Discontinuing and starting again                         126

Assignment                                               126

CPR 52.9A                                                127

Retrospection                                            130

Retrospective retrospection                              131

7.  **PART 36**                                          135

The idea                                                 135

The reality                                              135

Exercise                                                 138

Case Study      140

**8. DISCONTINUANCE, STRIKE-OUT and SUMMARY JUDGMENT**      143

Strike-Out and Summary Judgment      143

Strike out      143

No Reasonable Grounds      143

No Reasonable grounds      145

Oh What Tangled Webs We Weave      145

An Abuse of Process      146

Delay      146

Obstructing Just Disposal      146

Failure to attend trial      146

Failure to file Pre-Trial Checklist      147

Discontinuance      148

Discontinuance- Not as simple as you may think      149

Jumping the gun      151

Court's discretion to set aside Notice of Discontinuance      152

Discontinuance- CPR 38.6      154

Discontinuance and Fundamental Dishonesty      155

9.   FINANCIAL BENEFIT OF ANOTHER                                159

10.  MISCELLANEOUS                                              169

        Provisional Assessment                                 169

        Fixed Recoverable Costs                                169

        Does QOCS Apply To A Claim By a Defendant
        Against a Third Party?                                 169

        Is QOCS Legal, That Is Is It Intra Vires?              171

        Does The Existence Of Defence Junior Counsel's
        Pre-1 April 2013 Conditional Fee Agreement
        Mean That QOCS Did Not Apply To It?                    171

PART III – STATUTES ETC

11.  STATUTES ETC                                              174

        Criminal Justice and Courts Act 2015                   174

        CPR 44.13 – 44.17                                      176

        44.13                                                  176

        44.14                                                  176

        44.15                                                  177

        44.16                                                  177

        44.17                                                  178

        Practice Direction 44                                  179

**PART IV - EXTENDING QUALIFIED ONE WAY COSTS SHIFTING**

**12. EXTENDING QUALIFIED ONE WAY COSTS SHIFTING**      183

Scope      185

Procedure      186

Retrospection      187

Agreement      187

Statement of Assets      187

Severe financial hardship      187

Means      188

Modest means – full costs protection –
nil net liability (Draft CPR 44.22)      188

Mid group of some means –
partial costs protection – capped liability
(Draft CPR 44.23)      188

Reasonable Amount      189

Substantial means – no costs protection      190

Confidentiality (Draft CPR 44.26(3))      190

Variation or loss of costs protection
(Draft CPR 44.21, 44.24 and 44.25)      190

Retrospective Orders (Draft CPR 44.27)      191

Enforcement      191

Costs of Applications      192

Extending the scheme 192

The Draft Civil Procedure Rules 193

Further extension 197

**PART V SET OFF**

**13. SET OFF** 200

Case Law 202

Reid v Cupper 211

**PART VI REFERENCES**

**14. REFERENCES** 217

Statutes 217

Statutory Instruments 218

Civil Procedure Rules 219

Practice Directions 220

Case Law 220

Other 224

# GLOSSARY

**Adverse costs:** The other side's costs that is adverse to the person paying them.

**Aiel:** A writ which lies where a man's grandfather being seised of lands and tenements in fee simple the day that he died, and a stranger abated or entered the same day and dispossessed the heir of his inheritance.

**Assessment:** Procedure whereby the court decides what costs should be awarded. Assessment can be a summary, provisional or detailed.

**Basic Costs/Base Costs:** The amount the client is contractually obliged to pay to his or her solicitor, a part of which is recovered from an unsuccessful opponent in the event of a win. These costs are also known as Solicitor and Own Client Costs. The element recovered is known as "inter-parties" costs or "between the parties" costs.

| | |
|---|---|
| **Cap:** | An agreed maximum to be charged to the client. In personal injury work this is now normally by reference to damages. In relation to the success fee element this is a statutory maximum of 25% but in relation to all costs it is a matter of contract between solicitor and client. |
| **Civil Procedure Rules:** | Set of rules, constantly updated, which govern all civil proceedings in England and Wales. |
| **Conditional Fee Agreement (CFA):** | A creature of statute. A form of contingency fee that is subject to additional conditions laid down by Parliament. In return for agreeing to charge no fee, or a lower fee, in the event of losing, the lawyer is entitled to charge an additional fee over and above her or his normal fee, in the event of a win. The distinguishing feature of Conditional Fee Agreements, as compared with straight forward Contingency Fee Agreements, is that the lawyer's success fee is calculated by reference to the ordinary fee, rather than just damages. However the imposition of a cap on that additional fee effectively transforms conditional fees into contingency fees. |

**Contingency fee:** An arrangement whereby the lawyer's fee is expressed as a percentage of damages and is thus governed by the amount recovered and not directly by the amount of work done. Common in the United States.

**Cosinage:** Fraud, deceit.

**Novel disseisin:** Recent dispossession. This was an action to recover lands of which the plaintiff had been disseised, or dispossessed. The action became very popular due to its speed. Rather than dealing with the issue of lawful possession, it simply asked whether a dispossession had taken place and if it had the property was restored to the plaintiff immediately with the question of true ownership being dealt with later. It was dealt with at the assize of novel disseisin, which was one of three petty assizes established by the assize of Clarendon by Henry II in 1166 along with the assize of Northampton 1176 and these three petty assizes lasted until 1833. The other two were the assize of mort d'ancestor and the assize of darrein presentment.

**Costs following the event:** See cost-shifting

**Cost-Shifting:** Rule whereby the losing party in litigation pays the winning party's costs, or more generally, a percentage of them. Also known as "loser pays" or "costs following the event" or "two-way rule" or "winner takes all".

**Darrein presentment:** An action brought to enquire who was the last patron to present a benefice to a church then vacant of which the plaintiff complained that he had been unlawfully deprived by the defendant. The action was related to the aristocratic privilege of the right to appoint a parson to a particular parish.

**Demandant:** Old name for a claimant.

**Indemnity costs:** The full amount of the costs incurred by a party. Normally a party recovers costs against the other side on the standard basis, rather than the indemnity basis. Standard costs are subject to the concept of proportionality whereas indemnity costs are not. Standard costs are for all intents and purposes subject to guideline hourly rates followed by the court whereas indemnity costs are not. The award of indemnity costs has traditionally marked disapproval by the court of the paying party's conduct. However, and confusingly, indemnity costs should now be awarded where a claimant matches or beats its own Part 36 offer and that does not involve any criticism of the defendant. Because of the traditional association of indemnity costs with misconduct judges seem reluctant to award claimants indemnity costs where they match or beat their own Part 36 offer.

**Indemnity principle:**

Extremely complicated principle which expressed simply means that the losing party is only liable for legal costs which the winning party has agreed to pay their lawyers. This has traditionally been interpreted as making Conditional Fee Agreements or Contingency Fee Agreements unenforceable as the law does not distinguish between a win and a loss. Thus in the event of a loss the client had agreed to pay his or her lawyer nothing, so under the indemnity principle, even if the client wins and had agreed to pay his lawyers in the event of a win, he can recover nothing from the other side. This has always encouraged

| | solicitors to increase fees to justify recovery from the other side. |
|---|---|
| **Inter-partes costs:** | Costs recovered by a winning party from a losing party. Now correctly known as "between the parties costs". |
| **Legal aid:** | A form of financial assistance by the state for those of moderate means. Now abolished in civil matters with very limited exceptions. |
| **Loser pays:** | Rule whereby the losing party in litigation pays the winning party's costs, or more generally a percentage of them. Also known as "costs-shifting", "costs following the event" or "two-way rule" or "winner takes all". |
| **Mort d'ancestor:** | An action brought by a plaintiff who claimed that the defendant had entered upon a freehold property belonging to the plaintiff following the death of one of his relatives. |
| **Multi-party actions:** | Defined as cases where there are 10 or more people bringing a claim. |
| **No-way rule:** | Rule whereby the court generally makes no order for costs, that is each party pays their own costs, win or lose. In contingency fee |

cases this means the losing party has no liability for costs, either to his own lawyers or to the winner's lawyers. This system is in operation in the United States.

**Obiter:** A statement in a judgment not necessary to decide the result of that case. Consequently an obiter statement is not binding on other courts but is persuasive.

**One-way rule:** Rule whereby one party only is potentially liable for the other side's costs and one party is immune. This is the basis of one-way costs shifting.

**Part 36:** Technically Civil Procedure Rule no 36, but always known as Part 36. A rule of extreme complexity. Putting it very simply indeed where a defendant makes a Part 36 offer, and such offers are subject to considerable formalities, and the claimant fails to get more at trial than the offer then the claimant has to pay all of the defendant's costs from 21 days after the offer was made. This applies even in Qualified One-Way Costs Shifting cases and many commentators take the view that it wrecks QOCS. If a claimant matches or beats its own Part 36 offer at trial then the claimant gets indemnity costs, rather than standard costs, from 21 days after the offer was made and also a 10% increase in damages.

**Plaintiff:** Old name for a claimant.

**Practice Direction:** Guidance, which is not legally binding, in relation to the Civil Procedure Rules.

**Qualified One-Way Costs Shifting:** A system of one-way costs shifting, subject to qualifications.

**SCCO:** Senior Courts Costs Office. A specialist court consisting of specialist costs judges whose technical status is that of a District Judge. Nevertheless in view of their expertise their decisions carry more weight than those of other first instance judges.

**Small claims:** A more informal procedure in the County Court in which costs do not follow the event, that is that each party is liable for their own lawyer's fees and cannot recover them from the other side. The general small claims limit is £10,000.00 but in personal injury cases it is currently £1,000.00 and on 25 November 2015 government announced that it would be increased to £5,000.00. This will probably be from April 2017.

**Solicitor and Own Client Costs:**     See Basic/Base Costs.

**Standard costs:**     See indemnity costs.

**Success fee:**     The additional fee, over and above ordinary fees, charged by a successful lawyer in a conditional fee case to reflect the risk of getting no fee, or a lower fee, in the event of defeat. Also known as uplift.

**Taxation:**     Same as assessment. Assessment was the original term, used at least as early as the 16th century and to which we have now returned.

**Uplift:**     See success fee.

# Part I

# WHAT IS COVERED?

# Chapter 1

# Introduction

# INTRODUCTION

## History

The concept of civil litigation in its modern form stems from the Statute of Westminster 1275.

One-Way Costs Shifting was introduced in 1277 by the Statute of Gloucester (1277, 6 Edward I. c. 1), which provided that

"the demandant shall recover damages in an assize of novel disseisin and in writs of mort d'ancestor, cosinage, aiel and beziel, and further that the demandant may recover against the tenant the costs of his writ purchased together with the damages above said. And this act shall hold in all cases when the party is to recover damages."

"Costs of his writ" were extended and interpreted to mean all the legal costs in the action.

Prior to that costs were not recoverable, although the Attorneys in County Courts Act 1235 established the concept of paid advocates but paid by their own clients.

Thus from 1277 whenever damages were recovered, no matter how small the sum, costs were recoverable.

The law was codified in the Recovery of Damages and Costs Act 1278.

It was not until the reign of King Henry VIII in 1531 that successful defendants were able to recover costs, so One-Way Costs Shifting existed for 254 years.

The 1531 Statute (23 Henry VIII. c. 15) provided that

"if in the actions therein mentioned the plaintiff after appearance of the defendant be non-suited, or any verdict happen to pass by lawful trial against the plaintiff, the defendant shall have judgment to recover his costs against the plaintiff, to be assessed and taxed at the discretion of the court, and shall have such process and execution for the recovery and paying his costs against the plaintiff, as the plaintiff should or might have had against the defendant, in case the judgment had been given for the plaintiff."

Cases in wardship in chivalry were an exception. The Statute of Marlbridge 1267 allowed successful defendants to recover costs in such cases.

However the 1531 statute provided that poor persons did not have to pay the costs of a successful opponent, so a form of Qualified One-Way Costs Shifting was established. It was that 1531 model that Lord Justice Jackson proposed in his report, that QOCS protection should be means tested.

That was rejected by the Civil Procedure Rules Committee. Wealth or poverty do not affect the existence of QOCS protection under CPR 44.13-44.17 of the Civil Procedure Rules.

Thus poor people remained immune to adverse costs orders, and that remained the case until the 19th century.

As for their own costs, poor persons could rely on the Poor Persons Act 1495 which exempted the poor from court fees and assigned lawyers to prepare pleadings and represent poor people free of charge.


A similar system had been in place in Scotland since 1488.

Thus there was a legal aid system from the 15th century until it was scrapped in the 19th century and replaced by an in forma pauperis procedure codified by the Forma Pauperis Act 1893. That applied only to the superior courts and remained in force as far as proceedings in the House of Lords were concerned until 1960, as the Legal Aid Act 1949 did not cover appeals to the House of Lords.

Thus as far as protection from adverse costs is concerned poor persons *have not been in such a weak position since the start of modern litigation 741 years ago.*

It is true that non poor persons now enjoy greater protection against adverse costs than they have since 1531.

As far as legal representation is concerned poor people are now in a worse position than at any time since the original creation of legal aid in 1495 (1488 in Scotland), apart from a brief period from the 19th century until 1949.

So from 1531 costs followed the event, with limited exceptions which were removed in 1606 by the Statute of 4 James I. c 3.

The policy of these enactments was expressed to be the discouragement of frivolous and unjust suits, no doubt at the behest of the Slave and Serf Owners Federation, or whatever then was the equivalent of the Association of British Insurers.

Proportionality was first introduced in 1267, by Section 4 of the Distress Act 1267, still in force, which provides

"Moreover Distresses shall be reasonable and not too great."

In the intervening 749 years no one has improved upon that vagueness, although the Limitation Act 1623 limited costs to 40 shillings, £2.00, in slander cases where the damages did not exceed 40 shillings, (re-enacted in the Slander of Women Act 1891 as far as women were concerned), and by 43 Elizabeth. c. 6 that rule was extended to virtually all litigation.

In 1840, by virtue of Lord Denman's Act 1840, 3 & 4 Victoria. c. 24, 40 shillings became the first small claims limit: if you failed to recover at least that sum you got no costs.

The Statute of Westminster 1275 had provided for fines in criminal matters to be proportionate to the offence.


**Modern Times**

The 1531 model of Qualified One Way Costs Shifting (QOCS) was the one recommended in Chapter 19 of the Final Report of Lord Justice Jackson following a consideration of the issues in Chapter 25 of the Preliminary Report.

Qualified One Way Costs Shifting was introduced by the Civil Procedure (Amendment) Rules 2013 and the scheme is set out in CPR 44.13 to CPR

44.17 and the relevant Practice Direction is Section II of Practice Direction 44.

As the pre-Legal Aid, Sentencing and Punishment of Offenders Act 2012 (LASPO) cases tail off QOCS becomes ever more important. Relatively few cases have been decided so far as the existence of QOCS or otherwise is only determined at the end of the case (CPR 44.14(2)) and only if the claimant has lost completely or failed to beat a Part 36 offer.

Thus the case needs to be post LASPO *and* have gone to a contested hearing; the issue will not arise in settled matters, although it can arise on striking-out and there are several decisions already on this issue, as obviously a striking-out application can occur early in the life of a case.

Early indications are that judges are unsympathetic to losing or discontinuing or struck-out claimants and are working hard to disqualify losing claimants from QOCS protection.

One of the key justifications for disqualifying QOCS protection is fundamental dishonesty on behalf of the losing claimant and again judges are setting a low threshold and are finding fundamental dishonesty in circumstances which practitioners may find surprising.

It may be that so few personal injury cases are lost by claimants that those which are tend to be as a result of misconduct by the claimant, or it may be that the concept of the loser paying the winner's costs is too deeply ingrained in the judiciary to be easily dislodged.

Either way the illusion of QOCS protection, and the fact that it is dis-applied if a defendant's Part 36 offer is not beaten, is causing major problems for claimants and their advisers.

**Interplay with Section 57 Criminal Justice and Courts Act 2015**

Section 57 of the Criminal Justice and Courts Act 2015 came in to force on 13 April 2015. It also adopts the test of fundamental dishonesty; under the Act a personal injury claimant has the whole claim dismissed if there is fundamental dishonesty in relation to any part of the claim and thus a winning personal injury claimant is deemed to have lost.

Far from being able to tell a personal injury client that they are at no risk of paying costs, lawyers must now warn clients that even if they win they may be deprived of all of their damages AND be ordered to pay the other side's costs, almost certainly on the indemnity basis.

Instead of enjoying a uniquely privileged position, of recovering costs in the event of a win and not paying them in the event of defeat, personal injury clients are now in a uniquely vulnerable position because of <u>section 57</u>.

True it is that that only occurs if there is fundamental dishonesty, but early indications are that the courts are setting a very low threshold in relation to that test.

In <u>*Hayward v Zurich Insurance Company Plc* [2015] EWCA Civ 327</u> the Court of Appeal held that exaggeration for financial gain is fraud. It seems to be common ground that fraud is more than fundamental dishonesty, whatever that means, and therefore anything that is fraud must also amount to fundamental dishonesty.

Thus exaggeration of any part of the claim for financial gain means that the case is lost under section 57, with the claimant paying costs.

If the case is lost anyway, for example on liability or causation, then exaggeration for financial gain will deprive the claimant of QOCS costs protection.

That case is being appealed to the Supreme Court, leave having been granted on 28 July 2015. The case reference is UKSC 2015/0099. As at the time of writing it has not been listed. You can follow the progress of the case at <u>https://www.supremecourt.uk/current-cases/index.html</u> or on my blog: Kerry on QOCS: Book Update and links.

**Structure of the Book**

In Part I I look in detail at <u>Section 57 of the Criminal Justice and Courts Act 2015</u>, which is inextricably bound up with Qualified One-Way Cost Shifting and I examine the scope of QOCS itself.

In Part II I deal with the very many exceptions to QOCS protection, including where there is fundamental dishonesty, where a defendant's Part 36 offer is not beaten, where the claim is for the financial benefit of another and where a claim is struck out on certain grounds.

Part III contains the statutory material, Civil Procedure Rules and Practice Directions.

Part IV examines the proposed extension of QOCS to defamation and privacy cases, a very different model to the personal injury QOCS one.

Part V looks at set-off, which is of crucial importance in QOCS cases and for many personal injury lawyers is a little known area of the law.

Part VI lists all statutes, statutory instruments, Civil Procedure Rules, Practice Directions, cases and publications referred to in the book.

**This book will be constantly updated on my blog – Kerry on QOCS: Book Update and Links – see How To Use This Book.**

**Summary**

1. Currently applies to personal injury work only.

2. QOCS fully retrospective except where additional liability has existed (confirmed in *Wagenaar v Weekend Travel Limitedt/a Ski Weekend and Serradji (Third Party)* [2014] EWCA Civ 1105, and may even apply if an additional liability existed but no longer exists – see *Casseldine v The Diocese of Llandaff Board for Social Responsibility (a charity)* Cardiff County Court, 3 July 2015, Claim 3 YU56348

3. Failure to beat a defendant's Part 36 offer defeats QOCS protection.

4. Costs orders are always made in the usual way – the restriction is on *enforcement* of the order.

5. Costs orders are NOT limited to the amount of damages, but enforceability is, but that itself is subject to very many exceptions.

6. Claimant's pre-Part 36 costs may be eaten into, by virtue of the doctrine of set-off.

7. The court is NOT limited to making orders only when the defendant's Part 36 offer is not beaten, even where there is no dishonesty.

8. The client is liable for his or her own post Part 36 disbursements.

9. QOCS does not apply to a claim by a defendant against a third party – *Wagenaar*

10. A defendant's CFA with an additional liability does *not* de-QOCS the case – *Wagenaar*

11. If there was a recoverable additional liability at first instance then QOCS does not apply on any appeal, even if there is a fresh conditional fee agreement without a success fee in the appeal proceedings – *Landau v The Big Bus Company*, 31 October 2014, Master Haworth SCCO, although *Casseldine v The Diocese of Llandaff Board for Social Responsibility (a charity)* Cardiff County Court, 3 July 2015, Claim 3 YU56348 suggests otherwise.

    Both are first instance decisions and neither is being appealed.

12. Section 57 of the Criminal Justice and Courts Act 2015 undermines the whole concept of QOCS.

13. Early indications are that courts are setting a very low threshold for "fundamental dishonesty" - *Hayward v Zurich Insurance Company plc* [2015] EWCA Civ 327,- one of the key reasons for disqualifying QOCS and the only issue in Section 57 cases.

# EXERCISE

You act for a claimant in a case where you are reasonably confident, but by no means certain, of winning. You value the damages at £100,000.

    (A)  Under the old regime, with ATE insurance in place to cover own disbursements and adverse costs, including in relation to Part 36, what is the minimum Part 36 offer you would advise the claimant to accept?

    (B)  Does that figure change, and if so what to, in the new regime, with no insurance in place and no counsel on board under a CFA and a claimant who will be unable to pay counsel's fees, court fees and experts' fees in the event of failing to beat the Part 36 offer?

If you act for defendants then state what figure you would expect to be accepted (A) now and (B) under the new regime.

One of the points being missed is the solicitor's risk of being left with a liability for post-Part 36 disbursements that a client who has failed to beat a Part 36 offer cannot, or will not, pay. This is bound to influence solicitor behaviour. There is no point in a client spending a substantial sum on after-the-event insurance to cover this Part 36 risk unless that client is likely to recover a sum that exceeds the Part 36 offer by at least as much as the premium, in which case why take out the insurance at all?

Thus the client who beats the Part 36 offer will always question why such expensive ATE insurance was necessary and the client who fails to beat the Part 36 offer will always think that the solicitor should have taken out such insurance.

The initial consideration as to whether to take out unrecoverable ATE insurance essentially to cover the Part 36 risk is not easy.

True One Way Costs Shifting has considerable merit and operates in some states of the United States of America in relation to discrimination claims. Qualified One Way Costs Shifting with Part 36 remaining fully in force is unworkable, forcing claimants, to settle for less than before or to fund expensive after-the-event insurance.

11

Either way claimants will be left out of pocket, and that is without taking in to account the fact that they will now have to pay some of their own costs, generally a sum equal to 25% of general damages and past special damages, net of Compensation Recovery Unit payments, by way of a success fee.

# Chapter 2

## Scope

# SCOPE

In this chapter I consider the potential scope of QOCS and of Section 57 of the Criminal Justice and Courts Act 2015. Even if a case is potentially covered by QOCS there are very many exclusions from protection which I look at in separate chapters in Part II.

As the issue of scope involves a detailed analysis of what is meant by "personal injury" and as the applicability of the 10% Simmons v Castle general damages uplift involves many of the same issues, I deal with that as well.

## Type of work

The current Qualified One Way Costs Shifting scheme covers all personal injury work without exception, but nothing else. All relevant cases, irrespective of the parties' financial circumstances, are covered.

CPR 44.13 states:

"(1)    This Section applies to proceedings which include a claim for damages –

    (a)  for personal injuries;

    (b)  under the Fatal Accidents Act 1976; or

(c) which arises out of death or personal injury and survives for the benefit of an estate by virtue of section 1(1) of the Law Reform (Miscellaneous Provisions) Act 1934,

but does not apply to applications pursuant to section 33 of the Senior Courts Act 1981 or section 52 of the County Courts Act 1984 (applications for pre-action disclosure), or where rule 44.17 applies.

(2) In this Section, "claimant" means a person bringing a claim to which this Section applies or an estate on behalf of which such a claim is brought, and includes a person making a counterclaim or an additional claim,"

Section 57 applies "on a claim for damages in respect of personal injury" and by section 57 (8)"personal injury" includes any disease and any other impairment of a person's physical or mental condition.

**Issued Proceedings In England & Wales**

QOCS applies to proceedings issued in England and Wales. It does not apply until and unless proceedings are issued as until then there is no liability for costs and no entitlement to costs, and therefore no role for costs to play.

This lack of costs if proceedings are not issued is the reason any pre-issue settlement needs to provide, as a matter of contract, for costs to be paid.

Once proceedings are issued then there is an entitlement to costs and a potential liability for costs and in both cases that then includes pre-issue costs.

Section 57 applies to personal injury proceedings issued in England and Wales on or after 13 April 2015.

## Place of Injury

It is irrelevant where the injury took place. If proceedings are issued in England and Wales then QOCS applies, subject to the many exceptions dealt with later.

If proceedings are issued in any other jurisdiction, even if the accident took place in England and Wales, then QOCS does not apply.

The position is exactly the same with section 57.

## Date of injury

The date of the injury is irrelevant. QOCS is fully retrospective and could cover an accident that happened 10 or 20 years ago, long before the idea of the re-introduction of QOCS existed.

This was confirmed by the Court of Appeal in Wagenaar Weekend Travel Ltd t/a Ski Weekend and Serradji (Third Party) [2014] EWCA Civ 1105.

Most, but not all, pre-1 April 2013 cases will have a pre-Jackson funding arrangement with an additional liability and so are liable to be disqualified on that ground.

I deal with this complex issue below in Chapter 6: Pre-Jackson Funding Arrangements but it should be noted that it is the existence of such a funding arrangement, not the age of the case itself, that takes it out of QOCS.

A 30 year old case with no Pre-Jackson Funding Arrangement is covered by QOCS.

Section 57 applies to any personal injury claim issued on or after 13 April 2015 and the date of injury is irrelevant.

**Pre-Action Disclosure**

Pre-action disclosure applications under section 33 of the Senior Courts Act 1981 or section 52 of the County Courts Act 1984 are not protected by QOCS (CPR 44.13(1)).

Section 57 applies to pre-action disclosure applications.

**Hybrid claims**

CPR 44.13(1) applies QOCS to proceedings which *include* a claim for damages arising out of circumstances set out in CPR 44.13(1) (a) to (c).

There are no work type exclusions.

In other words any proceedings of any type are covered by QOCS if any claim for personal injury is included.

Pre-action disclosure applications are specifically excluded as are cases where a claimant has entered into a pre-commencement funding arrangement (CPR 44.17).

Thus it is clear that *any* claim which includes a personal injury element is covered by QOCS and the *whole* claim is covered, even if the personal injury element is only a minor part of the claim.

Thus a professional negligence action, or a credit hire action, which includes a personal injury element, is covered by QOCS.

CPR 44.16(2)(b), which I deal with in detail elsewhere, provides that orders for costs made against a claimant may be enforced up to the full extent of such orders with the permission of the court, and to the extent that it considers just, where a claim is made for the benefit of the claimant other than a claim to which this section applies.

Arguably this allows enforceability in full, with the permission of the court, of a costs order in relation to the professional negligence part, or, for example, the credit hire aspect.

CPR 44.16(2)(b) relates to a claim "made for the benefit of the claimant other than a claim to which this section applies."

Clearly this section does apply to any claim which includes personal injury. That raises the issue of what CPR 44.16(2) (b) can possibly mean. If the claim does not include a claim for personal injury then it would never have come within QOCS to start with and if it does include a claim for personal injury then it is hard to see how it can be "made for the benefit of the claimant other than a claim to which this section applies."

Practice Direction 44, 12.1 to 12.7, dealing with QOCS, is entirely silent on CPR 44.16(2)(b) and concentrates almost entirely on CPR 44.16(1) and CPR 44.16(2)(a).

The credit hire aspect of a claim may come within the CPR 44.16(2) (a) exception as being made for the financial benefit of a person other than the claimant or a dependent; a professional negligence claim would not.

CPR 44.16(2)(b) appears to be devoid of meaning.

**Section 57**

The section "applies where, in proceedings on a claim for damages in respect of personal injury...." The wording is less clear than in relation to QOCS, where CPR 44.13(1) specifically applies QOCS to proceedings which *include* a claim for personal injury damages. Nevertheless I am satisfied that section 57 does cover hybrid claims. If not, it would be a simple device to add in some other cause of action to avoid the draconian provisions of section 57 applying.

What is much less clear is whether section 57 applies to the whole of the claim, or just the personal injury element, and whether fundamental dishonesty in relation to its personal injury element infects the rest of the

19

claim and whether fundamental dishonesty in relation to a non- personal injury element of the claim causes its section 57 axe to fall.

*Specific issues*

A housing disrepair claim, or professional negligence claim or whatever, includes a personal injury element. There is fundamental dishonesty in relation to an element of the personal injury claim. Is the whole housing disrepair/ professional negligence claim lost as well?

There is fundamental dishonesty in relation to the housing disrepair/ professional negligence aspect of the claim. Does this affect the claim at all?

**Small Claims**

**Section 57**

Section 57 applies to small track claims as well as fast track and multi-track claims.

In practice defendants may be less likely to run fundamental dishonesty in small claims as the potential saving is slight and fundamentally dishonest claimants are unlikely to bring claims not exceeding £1,000.00.

However with the personal injury small claims limit due to rise from £1,000.00 to £5,000.00 by April 2017 both of those assumptions may disappear.

## QOCS

Generally in small track claims costs do not follow the event and so on the face of it QOCS has no application as there are no costs to shift.

It is not that simple. A claimant brings a claim which is allocated to the Small Claims Track. The defendant argues fundamental dishonesty. Under section 57 a claimant who would have won is declared to have lost.

A claimant who would have lost anyway loses the protection of QOCS if fundamental dishonesty is established, but normally there would be no costs order as the Small Claims Court is a costs free zone, so there is nothing to be protected against.

However CPR 27.14 (2) (g) allows the court to depart from the no (actually strictly very low) costs regime and order payment of "such further costs as the court may assess by the summary procedure and order to be paid by a party who has behaved unreasonably;".

It is hard to see how fundamental dishonesty could ever be anything other than unreasonable behaviour and thus in one stroke will trigger a costs liability in the usually costs free small claims track and deprive a claimant of QOCS protection.

QOCS can also be used as a shield by a claimant who would otherwise be liable for costs due to some other, not fundamentally dishonest, behaviour. However, as we shall see QOCS protection itself is riddled with so many exceptions that a court that finds unreasonable behaviour will virtually always be in a position to order enforcement of the full order even in a QOCS case.

It remains to be seen if a failed allegation by a defendant of fundamental dishonesty will be treated by the court as unreasonable behaviour by a defendant and thus triggering a costs liability in favour of the claimant.

Allegations of fraud or fundamental dishonesty are rare in small personal injury claims but that may change when the small claims limit rises from £1,000.00 to £5,000.00.

A pleaded allegation of fraud generally results in the matter being transferred to the multi-track.

However that is not the way section 57 or QOCS works. At a small claims track final hearing the defendant can allege fundamental dishonesty so as to defeat an otherwise successful claim or to defeat costs protection in an unsuccessful claim.

There would be no question of the matter being re-allocated at that stage.

## APPEALS

Both section 57 and QOCS apply to appeal proceedings.

### Section 57

A defendant may appeal against the court's failure to find fundamental dishonesty in a successful claim and a claimant may appeal against such a finding which has cost her or him success.

That is relatively straightforward although appellate courts may not think so when grappling with definitions of fundamental dishonesty and substantial injustice.

It is less clear what the position is if fundamental dishonesty is raised for the first time in the appeal proceedings. Generally new evidence that was available at the first hearing will not be allowed in, so a defendant who has lost and not raised fundamental dishonesty at the trial and appeals against the liability decision, or on quantum, will not be allowed to introduce evidence of fundamental dishonesty which was available prior to the trial.

Supposing however that the alleged fundamental dishonesty is in relation to the appeal proceedings themselves. For example the defendant appeals against quantum and the claimant seeks to produce new evidence to show s/he still cannot work and the defendant, for the first time, alleges fundamental dishonesty.

Can the court overturn the first instance liability finding even though the appeal is only in relation to quantum?

It would appear so.

## QOCS

QOCS only comes into play if the claimant has lost. Thus a claimant could appeal against being deprived of QOCS protection and a defendant could appeal against the failure of the court to allow it to enforce the full costs order against the claimant. Unlike section 57 that does not change the result of the case.

## Liability appeals

If a losing defendant successfully appeals against the liability defeat then it is as though the claimant lost at trial, that is the starting point is that QOCS applies unless defeated by one of the myriad exceptions.

If a losing claimant fails on appeal then the situation is the same: QOCS applies unless one of the exceptions come into play.

QOCS can never have any relevance to an ultimately successful claimant, so cannot come into play in the event of a failed defendant's appeal or a successful claimant's appeal.

## Quantum appeals

The problem for the claimant is an appeal on quantum.

If the claimant brings an appeal on quantum and fails then s/he will have an order made against her or him for the costs of the appeal. QOCS applies but even in the absence of an order allowing enforceability the defendant can get its costs, and thus enforce the order and sidestep QOCS, by the doctrine of set-off.

Thus the defendant can set-off its appeal costs order in its favour by deducting those costs from the damages due to the claimant and/or the costs due to the solicitor in relation to the successful win at first instance. I refer to the costs due to the solicitor; that is the reality but it is trite law that costs belong to the client and can form the basis of set-off.

I deal with the concept of set-off, both under the Civil Procedure Rules and the common law in Part V.

The short advice is that a personal injury claimant should be very wary about bringing an appeal on quantum and is arguably in no worse a position prior to QOCS as generally after-the-event insurance would not cover the claimant's own appeal and in any event the claimant is still the winner and after-the-event insurers do not pay out on winners.

**Defendants' appeals**

The real problem for a claimant is an appeal against quantum by a defendant. The same issues apply but with the crucial difference that a successful claimant can choose not to appeal but cannot prevent a defendant appealing.

For all of the reasons set out above the claimant who has his or her damages reduced on appeal is deprived of QOCS even if they have done nothing wrong beyond resisting the appeal and seeking to uphold the decision of the first instance judge and if none of the QOCS exceptions apply.

For all intents and purposes QOCS simply does not apply in relation to appeals on quantum, something which needs to be made very clear to clients.

The whole issue of set-off arises in every single case where a Part 36 offer is made and renders QOCS largely illusory, even before the seemingly endless exceptions come into play. I deal with this in Chapter 7 – Part 36.

Defendants will be reliant on getting damages and costs back by way of set-off. Consequently if there is any thought of an appeal defendants should ask the court for permission not to pay the full amount of damages and/or costs, but to withhold some money pending the appeal.

Faced with a choice of enforcing a costs order against a client who has had the damages or a solicitor who has had the costs it does not need a genius to work out which one the insurers will try first.

Let alone costs my view is that the defendant can seek recovery of the damages from a solicitor. Thus the appeal court reduces damages by £10,000.00. That can be set off against the first instance costs paid to the solicitor, but belonging to the client, causing the solicitor to hand over £10,000.00 to the insurer.

## Multi-party claims

Both QOCS and section 57 apply in full to multi-party claims. In relation to most of the exceptions to QOCS there will generally be no more problems than in single party claims.

The big problem is in relation to fundamental dishonesty, which I deal with in Chapter 5. Allegations of fundamental dishonesty are, for various reasons, likely to be more common in multi-party actions. One of those reasons is that defendants have more to gain in a multi- party action.

The key issue is as to its effect of one party's fundamental dishonesty on another party. What happens if the generic statement contains inaccuracies which could amount to fundamental dishonesty? Are all of the claims then thrown out? Who knows.

**Legally-aided cases**

Both QOCS and section 57 apply in full to legally-aided cases. Legal aid, unlike a pre Jackson funding arrangement, does not disqualify a client from QOCS protection.

Section 57 should not throw up any problems in legally- aided cases that do not apply in non- legally aided cases.

In relation to QOCS it appears that a defendant who successfully argues fundamental dishonesty in relation to an unsuccessful claimant, the only time that it can apply, does not thereby automatically get its costs. It will have also to overcome the separate legal aid rules which generally mean that a defendant does not recover costs, even if successful.

Clearly a defendant who establishes fundamental dishonesty is likely to succeed in enforcing a costs order against a legally aided- party, but the application still needs to be made and defendants should remember this.

The Part 36 provisions in relation to QOCS effectively operate in relation to legally-aided cases.


## MOTOR INSURERS BUREAU CLAIMS


### Uninsured Drivers


Uninsured drivers' claims are brought in the conventional way through the portals and courts and are covered by the Civil Procedure Rules and thus are covered both by section 57 and QOCS as with all other personal injury cases.


They are dealt with under the <u>MIB Uninsured Drivers Agreement</u>.


### Untraced drivers


Untraced drivers' claims are dealt with under a separate procedure with a separate costs regime and in my view QOCS does not apply.


It is arguable that such a claim is nevertheless "a claim for damages in respect of personal injury" and that section 57 applies.


However section 57 is full of references to "a court" and what the "court" must do and indeed this section only applies if "(a) the court finds that the claimant is entitled to damages in respect of the claim, but

(b) on an application by the defendant for the dismissal of the claim under this section, the court is satisfied on the balance of probabilities that the claimant has been fundamentally dishonest in relation to the primary claim or a related claim."

That cannot happen in an MIB Untraced Drivers' Agreement claim and so I am satisfied that section 57 does not apply.

Nevertheless though there is no specific provision in the Untraced Drivers' Agreement barring a claim due to fundamental dishonesty it is clear that in effect Section 57 applies in full to such claims.

This is because of paragraph 8 which reads:

"8. (1) MIB shall include in its award to the applicant, by way of compensation for the death, bodily injury or damage to property, a sum equivalent to the amount which a court–

(a) applying the law of England and Wales, in a case where the event giving rise to the death, injury or damage occurred in England or Wales, or

(b) applying the law of Scotland, in a case where that event occurred in Scotland, would have awarded to the applicant (where applying English law) as general and special damages or (where applying the law of Scotland) as solatium and patrimonial loss if the applicant had brought successful proceedings to enforce a claim for damages against the unidentified person.

(2) In calculating the sum payable under paragraph (1), MIB shall adopt the same method of calculation as the court would adopt in calculating damages but it shall be under no obligation to include in that calculation an amount in respect of loss of earnings suffered by the applicant to the extent that he has been paid wages or salary (or any sum in lieu of them) whether or not such payments were made subject to an agreement or undertaking on his part to repay the same in the event of his recovering damages for the loss of those earnings."

Thus if there is any fundamental dishonesty in relation to any part of the claim a court must dismiss the claim and award nothing.

The MIB must apply the law of England and Wales, and thus must apply Section 57, and must award a sum equivalent to the amount which a court would have awarded in applying English law.

As that sum would be nothing the MIB must award nothing.

**Qualified One-Way Costs Shifting**

In relation to the initial application there has always been a system of One-Way Costs Shifting in the sense that a successful applicant obtains costs, as set out in the schedule to the agreement, but an unsuccessful applicant does not pay costs.

## Appeals

The applicant has a right to appeal against the MIB's decision; as it is the MIB itself which makes the decision it obviously has no right of appeal against its own decision.

Appeals are heard by an arbitrator.

Under paragraph 24 (4) of the agreement:

"(4) where there is an oral hearing and the applicant secures an award of compensation greater than that previously offered, then (unless the arbitrator orders otherwise) MIB shall make a contribution of £500 per half day towards the cost incurred by the applicant in respect of representation by a Solicitor, Barrister or Advocate."

There is no power for the MIB to obtain actual legal costs, even if it is successful in the arbitration and therefore this is a full system of One-Way Costs Shifting, rather than Qualified One-Way Costs Shifting and therefore is similar to the regime that existed in ordinary civil litigation in England and Wales between 1277 and 1531.

As the MIB Untraced Drivers' Agreement is just that, a contract, it is not subject to the Civil Procedure Rules and is not subject to the disqualifications from One-Way Costs Shifting contained in CPR 44.13 to CPR 44.17 and therefore fundamental dishonesty in bringing an unsuccessful claim, or an unsuccessful appeal, cannot lead to the applicant being ordered to pay costs.

Paragraph 24. (2) of the agreement does provide that " in a case where it appears to the arbitrator that, having regard to all the surrounding circumstances of the case, there were no reasonable grounds for making the appeal or bringing the question before him, the arbitrator may, in his discretion, order–

(a)     the applicant or,

(b)     where he considers it appropriate to do so, any Solicitor or other person acting on behalf of the applicant,

to reimburse MIB the fee it has paid to the arbitrator or any part thereof."

This refers to the arbitrator's fee, payable by the MIB, rather than legal costs.

It would be noted that paragraph 24. (2)(b) is effectively an order for wasted costs against the solicitor.

**Summary**

Section 57 and QOCs apply to MIB Uninsured Drivers' Agreement cases.

Neither Section 57 nor QOCS apply directly to MIB Untraced Drivers' Agreement cases, but the effects of section 57 do apply in full.

## CRIMINAL INJURIES COMPENSATION AUTHORITY (CICA) CLAIMS

Such matters are not governed by the Civil Procedure Rules and are not subject to the usual costs regime and so QOCS cannot apply. They are governed by the Criminal Injuries Compensation Scheme 2012 made under section 11(1) of the Criminal Injuries Compensation Act 1995.

For the reasons given above in relation to Motor Insurers Bureau Untraced Drivers' Agreement claims I am satisfied that section 57 does not strictly apply either. However the effect of paragraph 110 (1)(b) is the same, and indeed is the fore-runner of section 57.

Paragraph 110(1)(b) specifically provides that a claims officer may require repayment of all or part of an award where the claims officer is satisfied that evidence received after final payment has been made shows that the applicant:

(a)…

"(b) has deliberately misled a claims officers in relation to a material aspect of their application;"

Paragraph 110(2) provides that the amount of a repayment under 110(1)(b) "will be the full amount of the award made to the applicant;".

It is hard to think of any fundamental dishonesty by an applicant that would not involve having "deliberately misled" a claims officer.

The penalty is the loss of "the full amount of the award."

So here you have the origin of Section 57 – any dishonesty and all is lost.

Paragraph 25 provides;

"25. An award may be withheld or reduced where the conduct of the applicant before, during or after the incident giving rise to the criminal injury makes it inappropriate to make an award or a full award…".

Fundamental dishonesty is clearly capable of being conducted "after the incident" which may make it "inappropriate to make an award or a full award".

In addition any fundamental dishonesty in a CICA claim is likely to lead to a reduction or complete extinguishment of an award. Paragraph 27 of the 2012 Scheme reads:

"An award may be withheld or reduced because the applicant's character, other than in relation to an unspent conviction referred to in paragraph 3 or 4 of Annex D, makes it inappropriate to make an award or a full award."

Fundamental dishonesty in quasi-judicial proceedings must potentially make it inappropriate for a full or partial award to be made.

The CICA clearly has discretion to reduce, rather than extinguish, the award, a power a court does not have under section 57, where it is all or nothing, although under paragraph 110 (1)(b) the whole claim is forfeited.

## DISCRIMINATION CASES

Personal injury is not defined in the Civil Procedure Rules dealing with Qualified One Way Costs Shifting but CPR 2.3(1) provides that "a claim for personal injuries" means proceedings in which there is a claim for damages in respect of personal injuries to the claimant or any other person or in respect of a person's death, and "personal injuries" includes any disease and any impairment of a person's physical or mental condition.

Section 57(8) of the Criminal Justice and Courts Act 2015 uses exactly the same definition as CPR 2.3(1):

""personal injury" includes any disease and any other impairment of a person's physical or mental condition;".

### Actual Injury

Employment Tribunals have the power to award damages for actual personal injury arising out of discrimination, including physical, but more typically psychological, injuries, see for example *Vento v Chief Constable of West Yorkshire Police (No 2)* [2002] IRLR 102 Court of Appeal. The ordinary civil courts have the same power in relation to discrimination in non-employment fields, such as the provision of services. Actual injury cases in the Employment Tribunal and in civil court discrimination cases would appear to be covered both by QOCS and Section 57 insofar as relevant, but in fact is it is not as simple as that.

In the civil courts the matter appears relatively straightforward – actual injury claims will be covered.

**Employment Tribunals and QOCs**

However the position in Employment Tribunals is less clear. There are generally no costs in Employment Tribunals and therefore nothing to shift. They are governed by entirely different costs rules and the Civil Procedure Rules dealing with QOCS – CPR 44.13 to CPR 44.17 - have no application.

Thus I am satisfied that QOCS does not apply to Employment Tribunal cases involving actual injury, let alone injury to feelings.

**Employment Tribunals and Section 57**

However on the face of it Employment Tribunal proceedings are capable of coming within section 57(1)…… "proceedings on a claim for damages in respect of personal injury…..".

As we have seen the duty under section 57(2) to dismiss the claim "includes the dismissal of any element of the primary claim in respect of which the claimant has not been dishonest". (Section 57(3)).

So, exaggerate your client's future loss of earnings claim and the safest case will be dismissed in its entirety if there is a personal injury element.

Is a safe unfair dismissal claim lost because of exaggeration of future loss if there is a personal injury claim for discrimination included, even though there is no exaggeration in relation to the personal injury element? The answer appears to be yes, just as an ordinary personal injury claim is lost in its entirety if, for example, the credit hire claim is exaggerated.

37

## Injury to Feelings

Is injury to feelings species of personal injury? Does it involve impairment of a person's mental condition?

## Shorter Oxford English Dictionary

### Impairment

No definition given.

### Impair

1. Make less effective or weaker; devalue, damage, injure.
2. Become less effective or weaker; deteriorate, suffer injury or loss.

### Impaired

1. One that has been impaired.
2. Of the driver of a vehicle or driving; adversely affected by alcohol or narcotics.

### Impairment

The action of impairing, or fact of being impaired; deterioration, injurious lessening or weakening.

### Impair

To make worse, less valuable, or weaker; to lessen injuriously; to damage, injury.

## Impaired

Rendered worse; injured in amount, quality or value; deteriorated, weakened, damaged.

Roget's Thesaurus gives the following alternative for **"impair"**:

Damage, harm, diminish, reduce, weaken, lessen, decrease, blunt, impede, hinder, spoil, disable, undermine, compromise, threaten.

Roget's Thesaurus gives the following alternatives for **"impaired"**:

Disabled, handicapped, incapacitated, debilitated, infirm, weak, weakened, enfeebled, paralysed, immobilised.

Roget's Thesaurus gives the following alternatives for **"impairment"**:

Disability, handicap, abnormality, defect, deficiency, flaw, affliction, disadvantage, problem.

Those definitions seem to me to be potentially wide enough to cause injury to feelings to amount to an impairment of a person's mental condition and thus to bring injury to feelings into the sphere of QOCS protection.

Injury to feelings awards are usually in the Employment Tribunal. There costs do not follow the event and thus QOCS is of no application, for the reasons set out above.

However injury to feelings awards are also made in the County Court where costs *do* follow the event; discrimination in relation to the provision of services is a County Court, not an Employment Tribunal matter.

My view is that the court could legitimately decide the issue of whether injury to feelings is a species of personal injury either way, although it is significant that the word "injury" is used.

Employment Tribunals have the power to award damages for actual personal injuries arising out of the discrimination, including physical, but more typically, psychological injuries. These are generally awarded under the "injury to feelings" head of damages. The appellate courts have frequently said that there is no fine line between actual psychological injuries and injuries to feelings.

For example, in *Birmingham City Council v Jaddoo* UKEAT/0448/04/LA

the Employment Appeal Tribunal referred to "the inevitable overlap between injury to feelings and psychiatric damages….." (Paragraph 31).

In *Vento v Chief Constable of West Yorkshire Police (No 2)* IRLR 102 the Court of Appeal said that tribunals should have "……regard…..to the overall magnitude of the sum total of the award for compensation for non-pecuniary loss made under the various headings of injury to feelings, psychiatric damage and aggravated damages" such that "in particular, double recovery should be avoided by taking appropriate account of the overlap between the individual heads of damage".

In *HM Prison Service v Salmon* [2001] IRLR 425 the Employment Appeal Tribunal said that it is "necessary to stand back and consider the non-pecuniary award as a whole".

On balance my view is that injury to feelings should be classed as a species of personal injury and that cases involving claims for injury to feelings should attract the protection of Qualified One Way Cost Shifting in the civil courts, but not in Employment Tribunals.

In *Timothy James Consulting Ltd v Wilton* [2015] IRLR 368 EAT

the Employment Appeal Tribunal overturned the decision of the Employment Tribunal that had made an award of £10,000.00 for injury to feelings but had then grossed it up to take into account income tax at the rate of 40% and thus awarded £16,666.00.

There was no dispute that £10,000.00 was the correct figure; the issue was whether it should be grossed up to take into account tax and thus the real issue was whether injury to feelings awards are taxable.

Historically it had always been assumed that such awards were free of income tax and the current legislation is the Income Tax (Earnings and Pensions) Act 2003 and section 406 provides:-

"This Chapter does not apply to a payment or other benefit provided—

      (a)      in connection with the termination of employment by the death of an employee, or

(b)       on account of injury to, or disability of, an employee."

This replaced, and is a similar wording to, section 148 of the Income and Corporation Taxes Act 1988.

Here the Employment Appeal Tribunal carried out an exhaustive analysis of the authorities.

The Employment Appeal Tribunal said that the reasoning of the Employment Appeal Tribunal in the case of *Orthet Ltd v Vince-Cain* [2004] IRLR 857 EAT was persuasive and was preferable to a decision in the First Tier Tribunal (Tax Chamber) in *Moorthy v Commissioners for HM Revenue and Customs* [2015] IRLR 4 UKFTT which had held that awards for injury to feelings were taxable.

Consequently the Employment Appeal Tribunal held that injury to feelings awards are not taxable and therefore reduced the award back to £10,000.00.

It was a necessary part of the reasoning here, and in the Orthet case, that "injury" could include the concept of injury to feelings.

This reasoning was necessary because of the wording of section 406 set out above which exempts payments made "on account of injury to, or disability of, an employee".

There is no reference there to injury to feelings and therefore to come within that definition the Employment Appeal Tribunal here and in Orthet held that "injury" includes injury to feelings, or to put it another way injury to feelings is a species of personal injury itself.

Thus here the Employment Appeal Tribunal, at least equal in standing to the High Court, held that injury to feelings is an injury.

However the feedback that I am getting from practitioners in discrimination cases in the civil courts is that those courts are not treating injury to feelings as personal injury and thus are not providing QOCS protection.

In *Black v Arriva North East Limited* [2014] EWCA Civ 1115

the Court of Appeal rejected an application for a costs capping order.

Here, the appellant appealed against a judgment in a disability discrimination case but had not taken out a sufficient level of After-the-Event insurance before such insurance became unrecoverable by virtue of the Legal Aid, Sentencing and Punishment of Offenders Act 2012. Thus any fresh premium, to cover the increased level of cover required, would not be recoverable.

Consequently the appellant sought to have Arriva's costs capped at £50,000.00.

The Court of Appeal pointed out that this would now apply to all new cases as a result of Parliament ending recoverability of After-the-Event insurance premiums by means of the Legal Aid, Sentencing and Punishment of Offenders Act 2012.

"So the argument could be raised in any appeal brought in respect of a case under that Act. Such a result is difficult to square with the indication in the Practice Direction that an order for costs capping should only be made in exceptional circumstances" (paragraph 12).

The Court of Appeal also pointed out that it is not a function of costs capping orders to remedy the problems of access to finance for litigation. "If for instance, the respondent's costs were agreed to be proportionate, it would not be possible to exercise any jurisdiction to make a costs capping order simply because without it the appeal would not continue to be financially viable."

That is because CPR 3.19(5) (b) only allows a costs capping order if "there is a substantial risk that without such an order costs will be disproportionately incurred;"

There were other fact- specific reasons for refusing a costs capping order in this case but they do not establish any new legal principles.

Interestingly one of the submissions made in favour of a costs capping order, but rejected, was that there was a lacuna in the law in that Qualified One-Way Costs Shifting applied in personal injury cases but not Equality Act cases. As this is a disability discrimination claim in relation to the provision of services one would expect damages for injuries to feelings to be available. The issue as to whether such damages are in fact damages for personal injuries, and thus covered by QOCS, does not appear to have been considered in this case.

"Another factor was that the potential subject of the Costs Capping Order – Arriva – had already incurred vastly more costs than £50,000.00 prior to the application being made and therefore the Costs Capping Order would have been retrospective:-

"The effect of what I have described is that by the time of the application, the major part of the solicitor's costs of the appeal had been incurred. The effect of the order sought would, therefore, be that the Respondents will have already spent what is, if the costs capping order is made, in substance a budget laid down by the court without knowing that it had to stick to that insofar as it sought to recover its costs. In principle, the person who is the subject of the costs capping order ought, so far as possible, to know the budget to which he must work in advance." (Paragraph 25).

## Summary

### QOCS

QOCS protection is of no relevance in Employment Tribunals, either in relation to actual injury or injury to feelings.

### Section 57

Applies to actual injury cases in civil courts arising out of discrimination.

May apply to injury to feelings cases in civil courts arising out of discrimination. – see the discussion of what is "injury" in *Timothy James Consulting Ltd v Wilton* [2015] IRLR 368 EAT.

Appears to apply to actual injury cases in Employment Tribunals arising out of discrimination.

May apply to injury to feelings cases in Employment Tribunals – see the discussion what is injury in *Timothy James Consulting Ltd v Wilton* [2015] IRLR 368 EAT.

Logically, in relation to injury to feelings awards, either both section 57 and QOCS apply in the civil courts or neither do. The *Simmons v Castle* [2012] EWCA Civ 1039 10% uplift is subject to different reasoning, which I consider below.

### Children's cases

Section 57 and QOCS apply in full to claims by children just as they do to any other personal injury claim.

### Those lacking capacity

Section 57 and QOCS apply to claims brought by those lacking capacity just as they do to any other personal injury claim.

### Costs proceedings

Section 57 and QOCS apply to costs proceedings as well as to the main proceedings. It is trite law that costs belong to the client and that assessment proceedings, although almost invariably in personal injury claims for the benefit of the lawyers only, are in the names of the parties.

Does that mean that fundamental dishonesty during the assessment proceedings can lead to the dismissal of the whole claim? On the face of it that is the case. However that may be one of the instances where a court would find that it would cause substantial injustice to deprive a claimant of all of her or his damages, no doubt already paid to the client, due to the solicitor's fundamental dishonesty in claiming costs.

In the unlikely scenario that the client is involved in the fundamental dishonesty in claiming costs then it is likely that the client would indeed lose all of their damages.

An unanswered question is whether fundamental dishonesty in a bill of costs gives the court the power to disallow all of the claimant's costs. Arguably the court has that power anyway given its very wide discretion in relation to costs but section 57 undoubtedly strengthens that discretionary hand of the court if there is any fundamental dishonesty in relation to the bill of costs.

It should be noted with care by those putting forward the bills of costs that the Hayward case, discussed above, equates exaggeration with fraud and therefore fundamental dishonesty.

Many paying parties would contend that virtually every claimant's bill of costs is exaggerated and therefore is fundamentally dishonest.

**Simmons v Castle 10% uplift**

Actual injury awards in the civil courts attract the *Simmons v Castle* [2012] EWCA Civ 1039 10% uplift.

The situation in relation to injury to feelings awards in the civil courts is unclear, "general damages" awards attract the uplift and that is obviously a wider definition than "personal injury". My view is that injury to feelings awards being "general damages" do attract the 10% uplift in the civil courts. That does not throw any light on the issue of whether injury to feelings is a species of personal injury.

In Employment Tribunals the position is even more complicated.

There remains the issue of whether injury to feelings awards in Employment Tribunals attract the 10% uplift. Let us assume, as must be the case, that such awards *are* general damages and thus, on the face of it, attract the uplift. Why is there any doubt?

In *Chawla v Hewlett Packard Ltd* [2015] IRLR 356 EAT

the Employment Appeal Tribunal held that the 10% uplift under *Simmons v Castle* [2012] EWCA Civ 1039 did not apply to injury to feelings awards nor actual personal injury awards in Employment Tribunal cases as the rationale does not apply as successful claimants do not generally recover their costs in Employment Tribunal cases.

The case was unusual in that an award for actual injury, as well as injury to feelings, was made.

The EAT quoted from paragraph 15 of that judgment where Lord Judge, the Lord Chief Justice said:-

"15. Thirdly the increase we are laying down… is attributable to the forthcoming change in the civil costs regime initiated by Sir Rupert as an integral part of his proposed reforms which were unconditionally endorsed and supported as such by the judiciary publicly, and it was plainly on the basis that the 10% increase would be formally adopted by the judiciary that the 2012 Act was introduced and enacted."

Here the EAT points out that Employment Tribunal claims are not included in the list of specific types of litigation dealt with in the report.

At paragraph 91 of the judgment the EAT says:-

"The rationale for the uplift… does not apply to litigation in the ET. Accordingly the 10% uplift decided upon in that case does not apply to increase guidelines in cases on injury to feelings in discrimination cases in ET's."

This is in conflict with two previous decisions of the Employment Appeal Tribunal:-

_Ozog v Cadogan Hotel Partners Ltd_ [2014] EqLR 691 EAT and

_The Sash Window Workshop Ltd v King_ [2015] IRLR 348 EAT

In *Ozog* the point was conceded but the EAT said that the concession was rightly made.  In *The Sash Window* neither of the advocates nor the judge appeared to have a clue as to what the Simmons v Castle uplift was about, with references to inflation, the inflation uprating in *Da' Bell v NSPCC* [2010] IRLR 19 EAT and that *Simmons v Castle* was decided because the level of general damages was generally low.  The Judge herself refers to the *Da' Bell v NSPCC* inflation uplift as being 4 years old at the time of the hearing here.

The discussion and judgment on this point in The Sash Window are woeful.

Chawla is a much better reasoned decision and in my view is correct.

It is also in conflict with the Presidential Guidance 2014 which makes specific reference to the Vento guidelines on injury to feelings as having been updated by *Simmons v Castle* at paragraphs 13 and 14 which state:-

"13…tribunals may award a sum of money to compensate for injury to feelings…

14. They follow guidelines first given in *Vento v Chief Constable of West Yorkshire Police*, which have since been updated by *Da' Bell v NSPCC* and *Simmons v Castle*, but are still referred to as the "Vento" Guidelines."

A previous decision of the Employment Appeal Tribunal took the same line as the EAT here –

*Pereira de Souza v Vinci Construction UK Ltd* UK EAT/0328/14, unreported.

## Summary

| | DOES QOCS APPLY | S.57 | 10% UPLIFT |
|---|---|---|---|
| Personal injury civil claims | ✓ | ✓ | ✓ |
| Personal injury Employment Tribunal claims | X | ✓ | ? |
| Injury to feelings civil claims | ? | ✓ | ✓ |
| Injury to feelings Employment Tribunal claims | X | ✓ | ? |
| Small claims | x | ✓ | ✓ |
| MIB untraced | ✓ | ✓ | ✓ |
| MIB uninsured | x | ✓ | ✓ |
| CICA | x | ✓ | ✓ |
| Hybrid claim | ✓ | ✓ | ✓ |
| Appeals | ✓ | ✓ | ✓ |

# Chapter 3


# Section 57

# SECTION 57

There is a very obvious overlap between Qualified One Way Costs Shifting and Section 57 of the Criminal Justice and Courts Act 2015 in that fundamental dishonesty defeats QOCS protection and also means that the whole of a personal injury claim must be dismissed, even if liability is admitted.

Thus fundamental dishonesty causes an otherwise successful claim to be lost; it also causes the claimant in an unsuccessful claim to lose the protection of QOCS.

Section 57 of the Criminal Justice and Courts Act 2015 came into force on 13 April 2015 by virtue of The Criminal Justice and Courts Act 2015 (Commencement No. 1, Saving and Transitional Provisions) Order 2015 (SI 2015 no. 778).

I set out the section at the end of this piece, but the key provision is Section 57(1)(b) which requires a court to dismiss the *whole* of a personal injury claim if it is satisfied on the balance of probabilities that the claimant has been fundamentally dishonest in relation to the primary claim or a related claim.

## Commencement

Under section 57(9) this section does not apply to proceedings started by the issue of a claim form before the date on which this section comes into force. As we have seen it came into force on 13 April 2015 and therefore if proceedings were issued on or before 12 April 2015 the Act does not apply.

Note that issuing proceedings is defined as "proceedings started by the issue of a claim form" and therefore the matter being in the portal prior to 13 April 2015 does not succeed in avoiding the new sanctions. In that sense the provisions are retrospective in that they apply to causes of action arising before the Act came into force, if proceedings were not issued prior to 13 April 2015.

Thus any unissued personal injury claim and any personal injury claim issued on or after 13 April 2015 is caught by the Act. The date of service of the proceedings is irrelevant. Thus a claim issued in, say, March 2015 but not served until say, May 2015 is not affected by the Act.

**Effect**

Sections 57(1) and (2) require a court to dismiss a personal injury claim where the claimant is entitled to damages in respect of the claim if the court is satisfied, on the balance of probabilities, that the claimant has been fundamentally dishonest in relation to the primary claim or a related claim.

Section 57(1)(b) says "on an application by the defendant…" However if the court suspects fundamental dishonesty it could invite the defendant to make such an application, or exercise its power to dismiss the claim as an abuse of process. A court which may have felt reluctant in the past to utilize such a draconian power may feel empowered, or even required, by section 57 to take such a course of action.

Section 57(3) makes it clear that this "includes the dismissal of any element of the primary claim in respect of which the claimant has not been dishonest."

Thus fundamental dishonesty in relation to, for example, an aspect of future special damages means that the whole case, including the general damages claim, is lost. Likewise an exaggeration of symptoms, if that is held to be fundamental dishonesty, means that a client loses the whole claim including the claim for his written-off vehicle caused by the other party's negligence.

## Related claim

A related claim is a claim for personal injury which is made in connection with the same incident or series of incidents in connection with which the primary claim is made and by a person other than the person who made the primary claim (section 57(8)).

## Substantial injustice

Dismissal of the whole claim is mandatory unless the court is satisfied "that the claimant would suffer substantial injustice if the claim were [sic] dismissed." Thus the claim is lost completely; it is not won but with a reduction or complete removal of damages, or a penalty in costs.

"Substantial injustice" is not defined.

I deal with this in detail below.

## Costs

If the court dismisses the claim it must record the amount of damages that it would have awarded to the claimant in respect of the primary claim, but for the dismissal of the claim (section 57(4)).

When assessing costs the court must then deduct the notional amount of damages from the amount which it would otherwise have ordered the claimant to pay in respect of the defendant's costs (section 57(5)).

Thus if the defendant's costs are £30,000.00 and the damages would have been £20,000.00, then the claimant pays the balance of £10,000.00 to the defendant.

Given that by definition there has been a finding of fundamental dishonesty it follows that an order for costs will almost certainly be on the indemnity basis.

The Act applies to Fixed Recoverable Costs cases as well as all other personal injury cases.

It also applies to small claims track matters, which will be significant if the personal injury small claims limit goes up from £1,000.00 to £5,000.00 as announced by the Chancellor of the Exchequer in his Autumn Statement to Parliament on 25 November 2015.

## Definitions

Section 57(8) is the definition section and reads as follows:-

"(8)    In this section—

"claim" includes a counter-claim and, accordingly, "claimant" includes a counter-claimant and "defendant" includes a defendant to a counter-claim;

"personal injury" includes any disease and any other impairment of a person's physical or mental condition;

"related claim" means a claim for damages in respect of personal injury which is made—

(a)    in connection with the same incident or series of incidents in connection with which the primary claim is made, and

(b)    by a person other than the person who made the primary claim."

**Thus it will be seen that the key terms, that is "fundamental dishonesty" and "substantial injustice" are not defined.**

The Oxford English Dictionary defines "dishonest" as "now, fraudulent, thievish, knavish."

## Criminal Proceedings

Section 57(6) and (7) are curious provisions which read:-

"(6)     If a claim is dismissed under this section, subsection (7) applies to—

    (a)  any subsequent criminal proceedings against the claimant in respect of the fundamental dishonesty mentioned in subsection (1)(b), and

    (b)  any subsequent proceedings for contempt of court against the claimant in respect of that dishonesty.

(7)     If the court in those proceedings finds the claimant guilty of an offence or of contempt of court, it must have regard to the dismissal of the primary claim under this section when sentencing the claimant or otherwise disposing of the proceedings."

I take this to mean that the fact that the claimant has lost her or his damages, and paid costs is a mitigating factor in the criminal proceedings which the sentencing court must take into account.

For a detailed analysis of the Parliamentary debates in relation to this Act see my piece Personal Injury Revolutionised: Criminal Justice and Courts Act 2015.

## Problem areas

1.  Uncertainty as to how courts will interpret "fundamental dishonesty" – see "Fundamental Dishonesty"- for an analysis of the case law so far in the context of QOCS disqualification.

2.  Uncertainty as to how courts will interpret "substantial injustice" – see below.

3.  Proportionate or issue-based costs orders – does the claimant have to pay the defendant's costs, even if say 90% of those costs were incurred in fighting the allegations of negligence or causation or whatever on which the claimant won without being fundamentally dishonest where the fundamental dishonesty is in relation to say a small part of special damages which took up only a small amount of court and lawyer time?

4.  Split trials - claimant wins on liability but there is a finding of fundamental dishonesty. There then has to be another full trial on quantum, even though the claimant has lost, in order to determine the amount that the claimant would have got had he or she won, that is but for Section 57, so that that sum can be knocked off of the costs payable to the defendant as required by Section 57(5).

5.  Interplay with Part 36 and QOCS – see below.

## Risk Assessment

Section 57 imposes a huge extra risk upon those acting for claimants. A case previously unlosable on liability, for example a person injured whilst travelling as a passenger, will now be lost if the claimant is fundamentally dishonest in relation to any part of the claim.

As we have seen there is no definition of fundamental dishonesty, but in a different context the Court of Appeal in

Hayward v Zurich Insurance Company Plc [2015] EWCA Civ 327

suggested that exaggeration amounts to fraud, and on the basis that fraud is at least as difficult a threshold to overcome as fundamental dishonesty, then exaggeration amounts to fundamental dishonesty, causing the previously unlosable claim to be lost.

I deal with *Hayward* in detail in Fundamental Dishonesty below. It is being appealed to the Supreme Court. The case reference is UKSC 2015/0099. At the time of writing it has not been listed.

A good solicitor should be able to spot liability and causation issues and take the case on with her or his eyes open, but spotting what might just be mild exaggeration is impossible.

**Success Fee and Charge to Client.**

Section 57 alone justifies a 100% success fee in every case and solicitors may now take the view that 35% or 40% of damages is the appropriate fee from the client, rather than the more usual 25%, especially if self-insuring in relation to adverse costs.

Note that it is only the success fee, not the overall solicitor and own client costs, that is limited to 25% of damages.

60

## After-the-Event Insurance

Section 57 causes major problems in relation to after-the-event insurance. A case where there was no liability risk, but rather just a Part 36 risk, will now have a liability risk. A case where a liability has been admitted can now be lost on liability at a quantum hearing if the court finds that there has been fundamental dishonesty in relation to any part of the claim.

Thus all quantum hearings are potentially liability hearing replays.

A claim is brought. Liability is admitted. Past special damages are agreed and paid at £40,000.00. General damages are agreed and paid at £30,000.00. There is a dispute about future loss of earnings and that issue goes to court and the judge finds that the claimant had an unrealistic view of her or his future career prospects and has been fundamentally dishonest in the future loss of earnings claim.

Bang goes the whole award and the claimant must refund the £70,000.00, although will be given credit for it in relation to adverse costs.

Admissions in personal injury cases are now meaningless.

After-the-event insurance policies are bound to exclude liability where a client is found to have been fundamentally dishonest.

## Self-insurance

Solicitors are allowed to agree with clients to cover the risk of adverse costs, that is to satisfy any costs order made against their client – see *Sibthorpe and Morris v Southwark London Borough Council (Law Society intervening)* [2011] EWCA Civ 25.

Such a benefit to the client entitles solicitors to charge a higher rate but this must not be a direct insurance premium. Thus solicitors may charge an increased hourly rate and cap all charges to the client, at say 30%, 35% or 40% or whatever of damages rather than the more usual 25%.

There is a duty not to exploit one's client and there is of course the market.

Solicitors need to take care in the wording of the retainer and in the funding agreement to ensure that they are not liable if the client is found to be fundamentally dishonest in either a section 57 context or a QOCS context.

Bad enough that the solicitor will receive no fee from the other side in what was apparently a dead cert case but to be liable for the other side's costs due to one's own client's fundamental dishonesty is a step too far.

## Client Care Letter Wording

Irrespective of the insurance arrangements clients must be warned in very clear terms of the consequences of exaggerating any aspect of the claim.

Here is the suggested wording:-

Add to "Your Responsibilities":-

**"You will not exaggerate any part of your claim."**

Below that I advise the following in bold:-

**"Please note that in a personal injury claim any inaccuracy or exaggeration by you or on your behalf in relation to any part of the claim will lead to the whole claim being thrown out with you being ordered to pay the other side's costs. This will happen even if you have already won your claim. For example if the court finds that the accident was the other party's fault but you exaggerate your injuries or the amount that you have spent then your claim would be lost. You will then be responsible for my firm's costs as well as the other side's costs. Such conduct on your behalf will invalidate any insurance policy."**

**This statement has a readability score of 61.7 on the Flesch-Kincaid readability scale meaning that it is easily understood by 13 to 15 year olds.**

I advise that all clients be seen by a senior lawyer at least for the purposes of explaining the effect and meaning of fundamental dishonesty and also for discussing funding. Obviously a careful attendance note should be made.

Although the client has to sign a Statement of Truth in relation to their statement I suggest a following separate statement to be signed by the client in the following terms:-

**"I have read and understood the statement that I have made. I have had any parts that I was unsure about explained to me and I confirm that the statement is true and correct in every respect. I understand that anything wrong in my statement may lead to my whole claim being thrown out and me being ordered to pay the other side's costs as well as my own solicitor's costs and expenses."**

**This statement has a readability score of 63 on the Flesch-Kincaid readability scale meaning that it is easily understood by 13 to 15 year olds.**

In relation to the Schedule of Special Damages I suggest the following be signed separately by the client:-

"I have read and understood my Schedule of Special Damages. I understand that these are expenses that I have actually paid or am liable for. I have had any parts that I was unsure about explained to me. I confirm that the Schedule of Special Damages is true and accurate in every respect. I understand that any inaccuracy in my Schedule of Special Damages may lead to my whole claim being thrown out and me being ordered to pay the other side's costs as well as my own solicitor's costs and expenses."

This statement has a readability score of 64.5 on the Flesch-Kincaid readability scale meaning that it is easily understood by 13 to 15 year olds.

The above statement can be adapted for a Schedule of Future Loss.

In relation to medical evidence I advise the following:-

"I have read and understood my Medical Report. I have had any parts that I was unsure about explained to me. I confirm that the report is true and accurate in every respect. In particular I have been supplied with an explanation of the medical terms and I understand all of them. I understand that any inaccuracy in the Medical Report may lead to my whole claim being thrown out and me being ordered to pay the other side's costs as well as my own solicitor's costs and expenses."

This statement has a readability score of 61 on the Flesch-Kincaid readability scale meaning that it is easily understood by 13 to 15 year olds.

The above wording can be adapted for any other reports obtained.

Solicitors may wish to have the client care statements in any Conditional Fee Agreement.

**Substantial Injustice**

Dismissal of the whole claim is mandatory unless the court is satisfied "that the claimant would suffer substantial injustice if the claim were dismissed." (section 57(2)).

It appears that this is an all or nothing provision, that is that the court must either dismiss the whole of the claim on the ground of fundamental dishonesty or, if the substantial injustice exception is made out, treat the claim as though section 57 did not exist.

In other words there appears to be no power to disallow say half of the claim. The wording of section 57(2) is:-

"(2) The court must dismiss the primary claim, unless it is satisfied that the claimant would suffer substantial injustice if the claim were dismissed."

Had Parliament intended the courts to have power to reduce the award but not extinguish it altogether one would have expected Parliament to say so, for example with wording such as:-

"The court must dismiss the whole of the primary claim, unless it is satisfied that the claimant would suffer substantial injustice if the claim was dismissed, in which case it shall make such order as it thinks fit, including awarding the claimant a percentage of what would have been awarded absent fundamental dishonesty." Or whatever.

This is the view taken during the debate in Parliament, relevant extracts of which I set out below.

## Level of Burden of Proof re Substantial Injustice

In relation to fundamental dishonesty the court has to be "satisfied on the balance of probabilities that the claimant has been fundamentally dishonest in relation to the primary claim or a related claim." (Section 57(1)(b)).

The level of burden of proof is not specified in relation to substantial injustice:

"(2) The court must dismiss the primary claim, unless it is satisfied that the claimant would suffer substantial injustice if the claim were dismissed."

This causes problems. One would expect the burden of proof to be on the balance of probabilities as the proceedings in question are civil proceedings. The counter argument is that in relation to fundamental dishonesty the Act specifically states that the burden of proof is that of the balance of probabilities, whereas here it is not so specified.

The counter counter-argument is that Parliament needed to make it clear that in relation to fundamental dishonesty – essentially a criminal concept – the civil, not criminal burden of proof applies. The criminal burden of proof is generally expressed as proving beyond reasonable doubt, a much higher burden than the civil one of the balance of probabilities.

As the name suggests the Criminal Justice and Courts Act 2015 is largely a criminal statute. Nevertheless section 57 is headed:-

*"Civil proceedings relating to personal injury"*

and is dealing primarily with civil proceedings, although section 57(7) does deal with criminal proceedings.

On balance, but not beyond reasonable doubt, my view is that the balance of probabilities is the appropriate test in relation to substantial injustice.

**What might be covered?**

It was pointed out in the debate in the House of Lords on 23 July 2014 that the whole section is designed to do substantial injustice, that is a claimant with a good claim has the whole claim dismissed because of "fundamental dishonesty" in relation to one part of the claim.

Lord Marks said:-

"...*the subsection works against the interests of justice, or certainly risks doing so, in two ways. The first is by imposing a presumption in favour of dismissal, subject to a modest saving provision that, frankly, is difficult to understand.*"

"...*the saving subsection, "unless it is satisfied that the claimant would suffer substantial injustice, if the claim were dismissed",*

*is very difficult to understand. On one view of justice, and the view of justice which appears to be intended by the proponents of the clause, if there is dishonesty, it is not unjust for the whole claim to go. If that is the meaning, how does the saving provision come in at all? If, on the other hand, it means that the interests of justice seem broadly to require the claimant still to get some of his damages, does that amount to a duty to dismiss or is it merely a power to dismiss, which is what my amendments are directed to?*

*"The second area where I believe there is a risk that justice will not be done is that the clause as it stands allows for no middle course—no way of allowing a judge to reduce the damages rather than dismiss the claim, where a reduction in damages is really what is required to do justice between the parties."*

This supports my view set out above, that it is all or nothing once a finding of fundamental dishonesty is made.

Lord Marks also asked the question as to whether, for example, claiming five bus fares when only one was incurred requires the whole claim to be disallowed in what could be a very serious injury case.

No example was given in Parliament of what might amount to substantial injustice.

**Children's cases**

If a litigation friend exaggerates on behalf of a child claimant a court might find fundamental dishonesty but also that to dismiss the claim would cause substantial injustice to the innocent child claimant.

## Claimants lacking capacity

A court might take the same view in relation to fundamental dishonesty by a litigation friend acting for an innocent claimant lacking capacity.

## Loss of huge award

It remains to be seen whether fundamental dishonesty in relation to a minor part of a claim, triggering a loss of millions of pounds to a catastrophically injured claimant would indeed mean that claimant gets nothing or whether the court would find that such a disproportionate penalty would indeed cause substantial injustice to the claimant.

## Other matters

Will it spread?

During the debate in Parliament Lord Beecham asked why this provision was being brought in only for personal injury claims and not, for example, for breach of contract claims, professional negligence claims etc.

## Cost to state

It was also pointed out that in cases of catastrophic injury – which is where the point is most likely to be taken by the defendants' insurance companies – the losing party is likely to be the tax-payer who will have to pay for the care of a seriously injured person where the injuries have been caused by a defendant tortfeasor which has got off scot-free, or rather has its insurance company.

Thus the burden passes from an insurance company to the taxpayer, exactly as it does with the proposal by the Chancellor of the Exchequer in his Autumn

Statement to Parliament on 25 November 2015 to scrap general damages in low value soft tissue claims.

## Fundamental Dishonesty and Costs Proceedings

It is trite law that costs belong to the client and that assessment proceedings, although almost invariably in personal injury claims for the benefit of the lawyers only, are in the names of the parties.

Does that mean that fundamental dishonesty during the assessment proceedings can lead to the dismissal of the whole claim? On the face of it that is the case. However that may be one of the instances where a court would find that it would cause substantial injustice to deprive a claimant of all of her or his damages, no doubt already paid to the client, due to the solicitor's fundamental dishonesty in claiming costs.

In the unlikely scenario that the client is involved in the fundamental dishonesty in claiming costs then it is likely that the client would indeed lose all of their damages.

An unanswered question is whether fundamental dishonesty in a bill of costs gives the court the power to disallow all of the claimant's costs. Arguably the court has that power anyway under its very wide discretion in relation to costs but section 57 undoubtedly strengthens that discretionary hand of the court if there is any fundamental dishonesty in relation to the bill of costs.

It should be noted with care by those putting forward bills of costs that the Hayward case, discussed above, equates exaggeration with fraud and therefore fundamental dishonesty.

Many paying parties would contend that virtually every claimant's bill of costs is exaggerated and therefore is fundamentally dishonest.

## SECTION 57 AND PART 36

A client brings a personal injury claim, part of which is exaggerated and therefore fundamentally dishonest.

The untainted part of the claim is worth, say, £10,000.00. The claim is for £50,000.00.

If the defendant makes a Part 36 offer of £10,000.00, which is accepted, then the matter ends and the claimant gets £10,000.00 plus costs and does not have to pay out any costs to the other side.

If the claimant does not accept the offer and fails to beat it at trial but there is no allegation of fundamental dishonesty then the claimant gets £10,000.00 plus costs to the date of expiry of the Part 36 offer, less the defendant's post Part 36 costs.

If the defendant successfully argues the fundamental dishonesty point then the whole claim is rejected, and the costs to be paid by the claimant are reduced by £10,000.00 to reflect the value of the "good" part of the claim. However the claimant has to pay the costs of the *whole* action, not just the post Part 36 costs, and gets no pre-Part 36 costs.

A defendant will always be better off arguing fundamental dishonesty.

Fundamental dishonesty in a *lost* claim deprives the unsuccessful claimant of the protection of QOCS.

Fundamental dishonesty in a *won* claim deprives the claimant of a victory but credit must be given in costs for the damages that the claimant would have got in relation to the "good" part of the claim.

## SECTION 57 AND PROPORTIONATE COSTS ORDERS

Does the claimant have to pay the defendant's costs, even if say 90% of those costs were incurred in fighting the allegations of negligence or causation on which the claimant won with the claimant being fundamentally dishonest in relation to a small part of special damages which took up only a little amount of court and lawyer time?

Supposing that at the liability hearing there is a finding of fundamental dishonesty to defeat an otherwise successful claim. The matter must then go to a quantum hearing so as to determine the level of damages that will then be set-off against the defendant's costs (Section 57(4) and (5)).

The defendant then spends a fortune on experts' reports which the court rejects as unreliable, even fundamentally dishonest. Who pays the costs of those? Does the claimant get costs, or credit for the expense of fighting successfully this aspect of the case?

Can the claimant make a Part 36 offer in relation to notional damages that they will never receive?

The otherwise successful claim is lost because of fundamental dishonesty. The claimant makes a Part 36 offer of £100,000 in relation to the damages that would have been received. The defendant fights at the notional damages quantum hearing. The judge finds notional damages of £120,000 to be set-off against the defendant's costs.

Can the court make a proportionate costs order? Can the court notionally, or indeed actually award the claimant the costs of that part of the case?

Supposing the claimant made an offer of £100,000 at the very beginning of the case. Is any credit given for that?

What happens if the defendant says that the claim is only worth £10,000 and the claimant exaggerates it from £100,000 to £105,000 and loses because of that. What is the costs order?


## Case Law

I am aware of two court rulings on fundamental dishonesty in the context of section 57, as compared with the very many rulings given on the subject in the context of disqualification from QOCS, which I deal with below.

In Manchester County Court in December 2015 Ikea failed in a section 57 allegation against grandmother Carol Ravenscroft. This is believed to be the first such case to reach court.

The claim was worth just £3,500.

Counsel for the claimant, Mr. Martin Littler, applied for indemnity costs and aggravated damages, which one would have thought would be a given but Recorder Mahmood, for reasons which have not yet been given, refused.

Mr Littler, correctly in my view, described that as a travesty.

"We talk of level playing fields but the present fundamental dishonesty rules are an exercise in digging up the pitch."

Sheffield County Court has also dismissed an allegation of fundamental dishonesty.

However AXA Insurance has succeeded in having a claim, which pre-section 57 would have succeeded in part, withdrawn with an order in its favour for £18,000.00 costs. (Law Society Gazette: 5 September 2015).

Its insured had notified AXA of a claim stating that their passenger had opened a door which made light contact with a neighbouring vehicle, a fact initially confirmed by the driver of the third party vehicle.

However that driver and his passenger subsequently submitted personal injury claims for cervical spine injuries supported by medical evidence showing a 12 month prognosis.

AXA pleaded in its defence fundamental dishonesty. The claimants then withdrew their claims and were ordered to pay £18,000.00 costs.

**The Irish Experience**

Section 26 of the Civil Liability and Courts Act 2004 requires the court to dismiss a personal injury claim in its entirety where the claimant knowingly gives, or causes to be given, evidence that is false or misleading in any material respect, unless dismissal of the action would result in an injustice.

It is clear that section 57 of the Criminal Justice and Courts Act 2015 is based on the Irish Statute.

Experience in Ireland has shown that the main reasons for dismissal of cases under section 26, when the claimant would otherwise have won, are:

previous injuries not disclosed

false loss of earnings claims

damaging surveillance footage

serious and material lack of truthfulness in giving evidence.

The Irish Experience is that, just as in England and Wales, very few claims present insurers with an absolutely clear case of fraud or exaggeration. In relation to section 26 an assessment must be made, often at short notice during the course of a trial, and that is likely to be the position under section 57.

In Ireland a failed section 26 application by a defendant is likely to result in an award of aggravated and/or exemplary damages.

It remains to be seen what view the courts in England and Wales take, but one would expect an order for indemnity costs of the whole action if a defendant fails on a section 57 application.

*In Farrell v Dublin Bus [2010] IEHC 327*

the Supreme Court of Ireland upheld the High Court's decision to dismiss a claim under section 26 where the plaintiff had discontinued the doubtful part of her claim and continued with the untainted part.

The plaintiff here had been in a bus crash which had undoubtedly injured her. She claimed ongoing loss of earnings and swore an affidavit in relation to those earnings and when challenged by the defendant's evidence she swore another affidavit and when it was pointed out that they were contradictory she discontinued the whole part of that claim.

The Supreme Court said:

"Where, as in this claim for particular loss, (in this case the sum of €343,000.00), is simply abandoned when challenged, it is inappropriate for a plaintiff to simply proceed with his/her claim as if nothing unusual has occurred…

"there is an obligation, in such circumstances for the plaintiff, preferably at the commencement of the hearing, to provide the court with an adequate explanation why the claim was advanced in the first place and when it was abandoned. Failure to provide such an action will often give rise to an inference that the claim was not bona fide".

Here no credible explanation had been offered and so the claim was dismissed.

This is likely to be the situation in England and Wales under section 57, that is that merely abandoning the challenged part of the claim will not save the rest.

*In Dunleavy v Swann Park Ltd. [2011] IEHC 232*

the court said that section 26 was enacted "to deter and disallow fraudulent claims. It is not and should not be seen as an opportunity to seize upon anomalies, inconsistencies and unexplained circumstances to avoid a just liability. Great care should be taken to ensure, in a discriminating way, that clear evidence of fraudulent conduct in a case, exists before a form of defence is launched which could unjustly do grave damage to the good name and reputation of a worthy plaintiff".

Here the plaintiff had claimed that she could not play golf although there was photographic evidence to suggest that she had been playing. She failed to disclose a previous road traffic accident in her medical evidence and failed to disclose a history of psychiatric problems but when the allegations were put to her the plaintiff impressed the judge and that is apparent from the Judgment and the judge declined to dismiss the claim.

*In Ahern v Bus Éireann [2011] IESC 44*

the Supreme Court of Ireland rejected an appeal by the bus company against the decision of the High Court in Limerick to award a 78 year old widow damages.

Mrs Ahern had been a passenger on a bus in Limerick when the driver had to brake heavily to avoid hitting a car which pulled out in front of him and she had fallen from her seat and been injured.

Liability was admitted, but the bus company disputed the nature and extent of Mrs Ahern's injuries, in particular her claim for a carer costing €177,000, a claim which she withdrew after cross-examination. The High Court awarded her €40,000.00 damages.

The bus company claimed that Mrs Ahern did not require a carer and had given false and misleading evidence by claiming that she could no longer travel alone. The judge said that if she had overstated the connection between her symptoms and the accident, this could be just "an understandable exaggeration". He said the need for increased care had not been deliberately exaggerated, and her evidence was not knowingly false or misleading.

While her history was "not precisely correct on every detail", it was "substantially correct" and overall she had been a "truthful witness, even if every detail of her narrative was not necessarily precise". "It was "both understandable and human" for her to attribute some of her loss of independence to the accident, rather than the passage of time."

The judge also held that section 26(1) referred to evidence, and not to information provided outside court.

*In Nolan v Kerry Foods Ltd. [2012] IEHC 208*

the High Court said that even where evidence is "somewhat fragile", and a claimant has not sought formal medical intervention immediately after an accident, a judge may decide not to dismiss a claim under section 26.

*In Nolan v Mitchell and another [2012] IEHC 151*

the claimant maintained that he was so badly hurt in a 2005 road accident that he had to give up working as an alarm fitter. He said that he also had to give up his hobby of car-drifting, but photographs and surveillance videos showed him still taking part in this hobby and throwing another man over the counter of a chip shop.

He also claimed more than €450,000 loss of earnings, although his P60 showed earnings of just €356.00 per week.

The High Court held that his loss of earnings claim and his evidence about giving up car-drifting were false and misleading and dismissed the claim.

*In Ludlow v Unsworth and Zurich Insurance [2013] IEHC 153*

the court dismissed a claim by Lisa Ludlow for injuries in a car crash in circumstances where she handed her car keys to her former boyfriend Darren Unsworth, but he was drunk and incapable of driving.

The Judge said that the car was probably driven negligently, and alcohol consumption was probably the major cause of the collision but that the claimant had told the court "some of the truth but stopped substantially short of telling the whole truth and nothing but the truth" and that a claimant "cannot play fast and loose with the truth, cannot tell some truth but not the whole of it, cannot tell a mixture of lies and truth and leave it to the court to try to winkle out the good from the bad".

*In Folan v Mairtin Corraion and others [2011] IEHC 487*

Mr Folan claimed damages for back injuries suffered when he fell off a scaffold at a housing development. He said that he had not been able to return to work or play sports and had attended his GP on more than twenty occasions since the accident.

The defendants claimed that Folan had been negligent and that he had not sent a claim letter within two months, as required by section 8 of the Civil Liability and Courts Act 2004.

Folan said that he could do light work as a carpenter but would not be able to do heavier and more demanding jobs and that his loss of earnings from 2007 to the end of 2009 would have been €31,200. However he admitted that, after the accident, he had used a friend's crutches and limped when visiting the doctor and had taken part in Galway hooker races for three months, had learned to scuba dive and had participated in a horse fair.

He had also worked full time for a windscreen repair company while being paid unemployment assistance, and had even done some roofing work after his fall.

The judge said that he was satisfied that the injuries from the fall were "relatively minor in nature", and that was borne out by the time it took him to consult a GP. He had not seen his doctor for more than three years before the trial, and his use of crutches and an affected limp at a medical consultation could only be interpreted as "a deliberate attempt to exaggerate his symptoms".

While Folan was a truthful person, he might be telling "something less than the truth" about his fall and its effect on his health and the judge found that his evidence was probably intended to mislead the court and was therefore dishonest and he dismissed the claim.

*In Meehan v BKNS Curtain Walling Systems Ltd and others [2012] IEHC 441*

a glazier claimed for damages to his heel after a fall from first-floor scaffolding.

CCTV footage showed that the claimant's claim was "wrong in important matters" and that the claimant's version of the accident in the pleadings and particulars was "fundamentally wrong".

The High Court said:

"Section 26 is mandatory. If it applies to the case, the legitimate parts of the claim cannot survive with only the false or misleading elements dismissed." The court was not entitled to "separate out the good from the bad" and therefore dismissed the claim.

*In Higgins v Caldark Ltd and Michael Quigley, Unreported, High Court, Quirke J, 18 November 2010*

the claimant's case was dismissed because he had failed to disclose in his verifying affidavit that his brother had paid him earnings of €40,000 through a limited company.

The court found that the claimant's loss of earnings claims were largely based on his false and misleading information and thus dismissed the claim.

*In Behan v Allied Irish Banks Plc [2009] IEHC 554*

the claimant claimed damages for loss of earnings after falling off of an office chair and she claimed that she had "no illness, sickness, disease, handicap, surgical operation or medical complaint, physical or otherwise relevant to these proceedings, either prior to or subsequent to the alleged incident", although "there had been relevant injuries and relevant treatment".

The judge found that the claimant had failed to disclose in her reply to particulars a number of injuries and treatments including pre-existing arthritis, a left knee injury, falls from a bench in a hotel and in the street and a gashed leg after hitting a filing cabinet.

The High Court dismissed the claim.

*In Carmello v Casey and another, Unreported,*

Damien Carmello claimed that he experienced numbness on the left side of his face following a road traffic accident but the defendant alleged that the numbness was due to another incident six months after the car accident, in which the branch of a tree hit the claimant in the face.

The claimant was treated for that injury in Limerick Hospital, but did not mention it in his replies to particulars, although he disclosed other past accidents and claimed that this incident must have slipped his mind.

The judge said that there was not "the slightest possibility that he would not recall such a thing. It would defy any credibility in a young man such as the plaintiff, and I simply would not believe him when he says that he does not recall it".

The judge held that the plaintiff had been "deliberately untruthful" and he dismissed the "substantially fraudulent" claim.

In Boland v Dublin City Council and Others [2011] IEHC 176

the court found that the plaintiff's account in relation to the circumstances of the accident and the special damages claim were less than truthful and thus dismissed the claim even though the court accepted that the plaintiff had suffered a nasty injury as a result of the negligence of the defendant.

**Criminal Liability**

It was not until January 2014, that is 10 years after the Act, that the first conviction took place under the Civil Liability and Courts Act 2004. This involved a claimant who knowingly gave false or misleading information to a solicitor at his home in an affidavit in personal injury proceedings.

# Criminal Justice and Courts Act 2015

*Civil proceedings relating to personal injury*

## 57    Personal injury claims: cases of fundamental dishonesty

(1)    This section applies where, in proceedings on a claim for damages in respect of personal injury ("the primary claim")—

(a) the court finds that the claimant is entitled to damages in respect of the claim, but

(b) on an application by the defendant for the dismissal of the claim under this section, the court is satisfied on the balance of probabilities that the claimant has been fundamentally dishonest in relation to the primary claim or a related claim.

(2)    The court must dismiss the primary claim, unless it is satisfied that the claimant would suffer substantial injustice if the claim were dismissed.

(3)    The duty under subsection (2) includes the dismissal of any element of the primary claim in respect of which the claimant has not been dishonest.

(4)    The court's order dismissing the claim must record the amount of damages that the court would have awarded to the claimant in respect of the primary claim but for the dismissal of the claim.

(5)    When assessing costs in the proceedings, a court which dismisses a claim under this section must deduct the amount recorded in accordance with subsection (4) from the amount which it would

otherwise order the claimant to pay in respect of costs incurred by the defendant.

(6) If a claim is dismissed under this section, subsection (7) applies to—

(a) any subsequent criminal proceedings against the claimant in respect of the fundamental dishonesty mentioned in subsection (1)(b), and

(b) any subsequent proceedings for contempt of court against the claimant in respect of that dishonesty.

(7) If the court in those proceedings finds the claimant guilty of an offence or of contempt of court, it must have regard to the dismissal of the primary claim under this section when sentencing the claimant or otherwise disposing of the proceedings.

(8) In this section—

"claim" includes a counter-claim and, accordingly, "claimant" includes a counter-claimant and "defendant" includes a defendant to a counter-claim;

"personal injury" includes any disease and any other impairment of a person's physical or mental condition;

"related claim" means a claim for damages in respect of personal injury which is made—

(a) in connection with the same incident or series of incidents in connection with which the primary claim is made, and

(b) by a person other than the person who made the primary claim.

(9)     This section does not apply to proceedings started by the issue of a claim form before the day on which this section comes into force.

**Civil Liability and Courts Act 2004**

Fraudulent actions

**26.—**

(1)  If, after the commencement of this section, a plaintiff in a personal injuries action gives or adduces, or dishonestly causes to be given or adduced, evidence that—

    (a)  is false or misleading, in any material respect, and

    (b)  he or she knows to be false or misleading,

the court shall dismiss the plaintiff's action unless, for reasons that the court shall state in its decision, the dismissal of the action would result in injustice being done.

(2)  The court in a personal injuries action shall, if satisfied that a person has sworn an affidavit under *section 14* that—

    (a)  is false or misleading in any material respect, and

(b) that he or she knew to be false or misleading when swearing the affidavit,

dismiss the plaintiff's action unless, for reasons that the court shall state in its decision, the dismissal of the action would result in injustice being done.

(3) For the purposes of this section, an act is done dishonestly by a person if he or she does the act with the intention of misleading the court.

(4) This section applies to personal injuries actions—

(a) brought on or after the commencement of this section, and

(b) pending on the date of such commencement.

# Chapter 4

# The Structure of CPR 44.12 to 44.17

# THE STRUCTURE OF CPR 44.12 to 44.17

## Restriction is on enforcement, not the order

Note that a full costs order will always be made against a losing claimant; it simply cannot be enforced without the court's permission in certain circumstances. Nothing in CPR 44.13 to 44.17 dealing with Qualified One Way Costs Shifting changes the basic law that a losing party has a costs order made against it.

This is why CPR 44.14(3) exists and provides:

"(3) An order for costs which is enforced only to the extent permitted by paragraph (1) shall not be treated as an unsatisfied or outstanding judgment for the purposes of any court record".

This does not prevent a credit-rating agency taking it in to account; it does stop solicitors and barristers from being struck off or disbarred as there will not be an outstanding or unsatisfied judgment against them.

This is hardly a satisfactory state of affairs. I for one would not like an unsatisfied court judgment against me. Why choose to do it this way, rather than limiting the order, as compared with enforcement of the order, to damages and interest awarded?

Might a future Government decide that which is currently unenforceable may be enforceable?

Can a client with ATE insurance insist on the ATE insurer meeting the whole of the order, even that element which is unenforceable? Yes, on the face of it, and ATE insurers will need to word their policies carefully to avoid this scenario; maybe this is likely to happen so rarely that ATE insurers will specifically include discharging the whole order, even the unenforceable element, as an extra attraction to clients.

Any which way having decent, honest, hard-working people with unsatisfied court judgments against them is not good for the rule of law.

Here I look at the levels of QOCS protection: full, none or defeated only with court permission. It is arguable that nothing has changed and that judges have full discretion to enforce all costs orders, thus rendering QOCS meaningless. Indeed the absence of recoverability of after the event insurance premiums, inevitably leading to a sharp reduction in claimants being insured, means that in practice claimants in QOCS cases are far more likely to pay costs than under the old two way costs shifting rule.

CPR 44.13 to 44.17, dealing with Qualified One-Way Costs Shifting, do not anywhere or in any way change the basic law that a losing party has a costs order made against it.

Throughout the rule the restriction is on enforcement. Thus a costs order should always be made in the usual way.

**Partial enforcement without leave**

CPR 44.14 limits enforcement of that costs order to the aggregate amount of damages and interest made in favour of the claimant, which is nil if the case is lost, but can, and often will, wipe out the whole claim where a claimant has failed to beat a Part 36 offer. This was a non-issue during the recoverability of ATE premium period: everyone had such after the event insurance covering such post Part 36 adverse costs.

The common law doctrine of set-off, as well as CPR 44.12, allows a successful Part 36 offeror to eat in to pre Part 36 costs to satisfy the post Part 36 costs. Indeed insurers, the effective defendants, can go straight for the claimant's solicitor's pre Part 36 costs rather than the client's damages. Some are doing so already.

In the first case that I am aware of D J Gill applied the CPR 44.12 set off against the claimant's solicitors' pre part 36 costs *first* and then looked at allowing costs against damages under CPR 44.13 to 44.17. I deal with this in detail elsewhere.

There is no doubt that QOCS has increased, not decreased, the prospects of a claimant actually paying costs in a personal injury claim in such cases.

## Full enforcement without leave

CPR 44.15 dis-applies that restriction and allows full enforcement in the usual way without permission of the court where proceedings have been struck out on any of the grounds stated in that rule.

It does not apply to all strike outs, for example it does not apply to a strike out on the basis of failure to comply with a rule, practice direction or court order. That is a ground for striking out under CPR 3.4(c), but does not deprive the struck out claimant of QOCS protection, unless it is also found to be conduct likely to obstruct the just disposal of the proceedings.

## Full enforcement with leave

CPR 44.16 allows full enforcement of the whole order but only with the permission of the court and only in the circumstances set out in that rule, essentially where there has been fundamental dishonesty or the claim is made for the financial benefit of another.

## Ambiguities

Thus the structure of one of the worst ever drafted rules is that CPR 44.14 limits enforcement, CPR 44.15 lists exceptions to QOCS where court permission is not required and CPR 44.16 lists exceptions to QOCS where permission of the court is required and the subheadings so indicate.

If neither CPR 44.15 nor CPR 44.16 applies then CPR 44.14 applies. That rule is ambiguous. Clearly CPR 44.14(1) allows a costs order made against a claimant to be enforced up to the extent of damages and interest awarded without permission of the court, but in a lost case that sum is nil.

However the fact that CPR 44.14(1) refers to enforcement without permission suggests that there can with the court's permission be enforcement beyond the level of the total of damages and interest awarded, which would allow enforcement in a lost case as well as other situations.

However if that is the case, what is the point of CPR 44.15 and CPR 44.16? They are otiose as by virtue of CPR 44.14(1) a court would always be able to give permission for the costs order to be enforced to its full extent. Indeed arguably it renders meaningless the whole notion of Qualified One-Way Costs Shifting insofar as it ever had any meaning anyway.

There is a further problem with CPR 44.14(1). It does not actually say that orders for costs can be made for any amount but only enforced without permission of the court to the extent of the aggregate amount in money terms of any orders for damages and interest made in favour of the client.

That is the general assumption. However what the rule actually says is:-

"....but only to the extent that the aggregate amount in money terms of *such orders* does not exceed the aggregate amount in money terms of any orders for damages made in favour of the claimant". (My italics.)

That reads that insofar as any order exceeds the amount of damages and interest it cannot be enforced even to the extent of the amount of damages and interest without the permission of the court.

I presume that that is not what is intended but that is what it says.

CPR 44.14(3) reads:-

"(3) An order for costs which is enforced only to the extent permitted by paragraph (1) shall not be treated as an unsatisfied or outstanding judgment for the purposes of any court record."

That would not be a possible scenario if CPR 44.14(1) is read literally.

Matters are further confused by Practice Direction 12.6:-

"In proceedings to which rule 44.16 applies, the court will normally order the claimant or, as the case may be, the person for whose benefit a claim was made to pay costs notwithstanding that the aggregate amount in money terms of such orders exceeds the aggregate amount in money terms of any orders for damages, interest and costs made in favour of the claimant."

CPR 44.16 deals with fundamental dishonesty on the one part and claims for the financial benefit of a person other than the claimant on the other part. Practice Direction 12.6 suggests that it does not apply to "ordinary" QOCS cases.

This may seem a point of extreme abstruseness, but actually it is critical.

The key is whether the court has power under CPR 44.14(1) to give permission in an "ordinary" QOCS case, absent striking out, fundamental dishonesty and the claim being for the benefit of another etc., for enforcement above the level of damages and interest.

If it does then what is the point of CPR 44.15 and CPR 44.16, or indeed QOCS at all?

It would mean that the court has full discretion concerning costs as it has in all non-personal injury cases and previously did in all personal injury cases.

However if CPR 44.14(1) bars *any* enforcement if the order exceeds damages and interest, then the claimant is off the hook, even for post Part 36 costs of the defendant, unless the order is limited to an amount not exceeding damages and interest.

Set-off could then never apply as there could never be anything to set-off. And what would CPR 44.14(3) mean? How can there ever be an order exceeding the enforceable amount?

The Practice Direction does not help.

Thus the claimant is awarded £30,000 at court and an order is made in the defendant's favour for £40,000, leaving an unsatisfied balance of £10,000.

May the defendant set this off against the claimant's pre Part 36 costs?

Yes, seems to be the clear answer. That situation appears to fall fairly and squarely with CPR 44.12(1)(a). Costs of course belong to the client, not the solicitor.

See below under "Set Off" for a detailed discussion of this concept.

CPR 44.15 then deals with matters where the full extent of the order may be enforced without leave of the court, and those circumstances are set out there. Again this is not the whole story as by definition a court will have needed to have made an order on one of those grounds, thus effectively triggering full costs enforcement without *further leave.*

CPR 44.16 provides exceptions whereby the full order may be enforced, over and above the damages awarded, but now only with specific permission of the court.

**Set-off under CPR**

CPR 44.12 reads:

> "(1) Where a party entitled to costs is also liable to pay costs, the court may assess the costs which that party is liable to pay and either –
>
> (a) set off the amount assessed against the amount the party is entitled to be paid and direct that party to pay the balance; or
>
> (b) delay the issue of a certificate for the costs to which the party is entitled until the party has paid the amount which that party is liable to pay."

The Practice Direction is silent as to the effect of this rule.

This raises the question as to whether even the claimant's pre Part 36 costs are at risk of being eaten in to to satisfy the unsatisfied element of a costs order in favour of a defendant when a defendant's Part 36 offer has not been beaten.

## Interim payments and CRU

Even where enforcement is limited to damages awarded there are potential problems. How is an interim payment already spent by the claimant, for example on medical treatment, to be recovered from an impecunious claimant?

What about Compensation Recovery Unit payments? In relation to success fees capped at 25% of damages in personal injury cases, CRU payments are specifically excluded from the Allowed Damages Pool, that is the solicitor cannot take 25% of any CRU payment.

However CRU payments are not excluded in relation to enforcing a costs order in favour of a defendant. Thus a claimant may be liable to pay a defendant by way of costs a sum including a CRU payment that that claimant has never had.

Thus the claimant gets £40,000 including £10,000 CRU. A costs order is made in the defendant's favour in the sum of £50,000. The defendant can enforce that order up to £40,000, not £30,000, without leave of the court, even though the only sum that the claimant notionally receives is £30,000. The claimant owes the defendant £10,000.

The position is the same in relation to interim payments. Supposing a defendant has made an interim payment of £20,000 for medical treatment which the claimant spends on such medical treatment, but then fails to beat the defendant's Part 36 offer. The defendant can enforce the costs order up to the total extent of damages awarded, including the already spent interim payment, without leave of the court.

A costs order can be made against a winning claimant who has beaten a Part 36 offer, but is found to have unreasonably refused to mediate, or has exaggerated, or whatever.

I look at all of this in detail in Part II.

# Part II

# EXCEPTIONS

# Chapter 5

# Fundamental Dishonesty

# FUNDAMENTAL DISHONESTY

The term fundamentally dishonest is used in section 57 of the <u>Criminal Justice and Courts Act 2015</u> and in relation to QOCS in <u>CPR 44.16(1)</u> and is extensively referred to in <u>Practice Direction 44</u> in relation to QOCS but is nowhere defined in the Act, Explanatory Notes, the Civil Procedure Rules or the Practice Direction. This is in spite of the fact that section 57(8) of the Criminal Justice and Courts Act 2015 is a definition section but chooses not to define this term, which is by far the most important one.

I deal with the whole issue of section 57 in **Chapter 3-Section 57 above.**

CPR 44.16(1) reads:

"(1)      Orders for costs made against the claimant may be enforced to the full extent of such orders with the permission of the court where the claim is found on the balance of probabilities to be fundamentally dishonest."

So the term originated in CPR 44.16(1) which became law in April 2013, well before Parliament debated and subsequently enacted section 57 of the Criminal Justice and Courts Act 2015.

It should be noted that under CPR 44.16(1) the burden of proof is that of the balance of probabilities, just as it is in section 57(1)(b) of the Criminal Justice and Courts Act 2015.

Note also that even though the disqualification from QOCS under CPR 44.16(1) requires there to be a finding that the claim is fundamentally dishonest it remains within the discretion of the court as to whether to allow enforcement of the costs order as it is dependent upon "the permission of the court".

Under section 57 the court has no such discretion; dismissal of the claim is mandatory unless the substantial injustice exception is found and again I deal with that above in Chapter 3-Section 57.

Having said that it is hard to conceive of a situation where the court has found fundamental dishonesty and makes a costs order as it is bound to do, but then refuses permission for the successful defendant to enforce that order.

Indeed it is hard to envisage circumstances where the court will not also order those costs to be paid and enforced on the indemnity basis. Practice Direction 44, section II, dealing with Qualified One Way Costs Shifting covers fundamental dishonesty at paragraph 12.4 in these terms:-

"12.4

In a case to which rule 44.16(1) applies (fundamentally dishonest claims) –

    (a)  the court will normally direct that issues arising out of an allegation that the claim is fundamentally dishonest be determined at the trial;

    (b)  where the proceedings have been settled, the court will not, save in exceptional circumstances, order that issues arising out of an allegation that the claim was fundamentally dishonest be determined in those proceedings;

    (c)  where the claimant has served a notice of discontinuance, the court may direct that issues arising out of an allegation that the claim was fundamentally dishonest be determined notwithstanding that the notice has not been set aside pursuant to rule 38.4;

(d) the court may, as it thinks fair and just, determine the costs attributable to the claim having been found to be fundamentally dishonest."

That Practice Direction is not without its problems. Paragraph 12.4 (d) suggests that the court may deny QOCS protection in relation just to the costs attributable to the claim having been found to be fundamentally dishonest, but that is a discretion so the court, which has to make a full costs order in any event, may order the unsuccessful claimant to pay all of the defendant's costs.

I deal with the whole issue of discontinuance elsewhere. Thus fundamental dishonesty has a different effect on different types of case:

## The claimant wins

If the claimant wins but is found to be fundamentally dishonest in relation to any part of the claim, or a related claim, then that win is overturned and the claimant is ordered to pay the defendant's costs, but subject to a reduction from those costs of the damages that the claimant would have been awarded on the genuine part of the claim.

## The claimant loses

The court makes an order in the successful defendant's favour as in any other type of case but then has a discretion as to whether to allow enforcement of that order at all, and if so whether in full or in part.

In both scenarios, that is a win or a loss, the court has a discretion as to whether to order costs on the standard basis or on the indemnity basis, but given that by definition there has been a finding of fundamental dishonesty it is hard to see any reason not to award costs on the indemnity basis.

Time will tell how the courts exercise their discretion but clearly the key issue is as to what is fundamental dishonesty.

In a different context the Court of Appeal has recently given guidance, but the case is under appeal to the Supreme Court.

In *Hayward v Zurich Insurance Company plc* [2015] EWCA Civ 327

the Court of Appeal overturned a first instance decision that a claimant should repay a large part of a personal injury award from an earlier settled action.

It will now be very difficult for the settled cases to be reopened.

Here the claimant had been injured at work and liability was admitted and shortly before trial the action was settled for £134,973.11, the insurer having argued that the claim was exaggerated. It settled for around one third of the sum claimed.

After settlement the insurers were informed that the claim had been inflated and they successfully sued the claimant for fraudulent misrepresentation and claimed rescission of the agreement. The judge held that the true value of the claim was £14,720.00 and ordered the claimant to repay the balance.

On appeal it was argued that the insurer had settled the original action on the basis that it was overstated and fraudulent and thus should not be allowed to reopen the case simply because it now had better evidence to establish one of the factors that it had taken into account when deciding to settle. To allow the insurer to reopen the case would make settlements difficult, if not impossible.

The Court of Appeal upheld those submissions. It pointed out that the contract was one to compromise a disputed claim and that the misrepresentation on which the claim for rescission was based consisted of some of the very facts averred by the claimant in advancing the claim. This was not a case of collateral representations designed to induce the settlement as in cases such as:-

*Gilbert v Endean* [1878] 9 Ch D 259 or *Dietz v Lennig Chemicals* [1969] 1 AC 170.

Consequently the defendant could not now have the agreement set aside simply because he could now show that the statements put forward by the claimant had been wrong.

"In deciding to settle the defendant takes the risk that those statements are in fact untrue (or, to put it more accurately, would not be proved at trial) and pays a sum commensurate with his assessment of that risk. He could have taken the case to trial in order to disprove the statements in question; but by settling he agrees to forego that opportunity and he cannot reserve the right to come back later for another attempt. If it were otherwise no settlement would be final." (Paragraph 16 of the Judgment).

By entering into the settlement the defendant implicitly agrees not to seek to have it aside on the basis that the statements made in support of the claim were false.

The Court of Appeal went on to say that the position would be different where the factual statements advanced by the claimant and replied upon by the defendant were not merely false but were fraudulent. However the court went on to say:-

"If it is in any case sufficiently apparent that the defendant intended to settle notwithstanding the possibility that the claim was fraudulently advanced, either generally or in some particular respect – the paradigm being where he has previously so asserted – there can be no reason in principle why he should not be held to his agreement even if the fraud subsequently becomes demonstrable." (Paragraph 19 of the Judgment).

The Court of Appeal said that it cannot be right that a defendant who has made an allegation of fraud against the claimant but decided not to have it tested in the court should be allowed, whenever he chooses, to revive that allegation as a basis for setting aside the settlement.

That was the case here.

Parties who settle claims with their eyes wide open should not be entitled to revive them only because better evidence comes along later. Here Zurich had alleged fraud from the outset and what happened afterwards was that better evidence of that fraud came to light after the settlement contract had been made.

At paragraph 33 the court said:-

"To extend the law of rescission in the manner here under consideration would have the most unfortunate consequences. The first would be that it would become almost impossible to compromise a whole swathe of litigation if settlements were vulnerable to being set aside in this manner. Apprehension by one party that his opponent may persuade the trial judge of matters which he denies, and disbelieves, is an everyday characteristic of litigation, and a healthy driver towards settlement, as every mediator knows. If the principle contended for were correct, almost any litigant could say that he was influenced to settle a case for more than it was worth because of a fear that the judge might believe his opponent, even though he did not. To be able to treat as an actionable misrepresentation the opponent's statement of his case merely because of such an everyday apprehension would expose almost any settlement to subsequent attack if fresh evidence became available. Indeed, there is nothing in the reliance test propounded by the judge that would even make the obtaining of fresh evidence a necessary condition. The public policy which encourages settlement of litigation would be gravely undermined if, in effect, dissatisfaction on either side led, with or without later forensic research, to the settlement being impugned on the ground that the opponent's case contained a misrepresentation which, without being believed, influenced the terms of settlement."

This case would have been decided differently had the new section 57 of the Criminal Justice and Courts Act 2015 been in force at the time.

The court clearly found fundamental dishonesty, indeed fraud, and therefore there could have been no question of any part of the claim being allowed to stand; the whole claim would have had to have been dismissed, even though the defendant was liable for part of the damages.

The case is potentially significant in relation to the definition of fundamental dishonesty, both in relation to section 57 and also in relation to Qualified One-Way Costs Shifting.

Working on the basis that anything that constitutes fraud has also passed the fundamental dishonesty test, that is assuming that fundamental dishonestly is in fact a step short of fraud, then any exaggeration for financial gain will constitute fundamental dishonesty and thus trigger the loss of Qualified One-Way Costs Shifting protection and also the loss of the whole claim which otherwise would have been successful.

Here the allegation of the defence was as follows:-

"The Claimant has exaggerated his difficulties in recovery and current physical condition for financial gain."

There was no direct reference to fraud or dishonesty.

Indeed the whole point of the second action was that they had now discovered that the claimant had acted fraudulently and they had not taken that into account when setting the first action.

Here the court said, at paragraph 20:-

"The employers had in their Defence not simply put them in issue but positively asserted that they were dishonestly advanced: see para. 2 above. Ms Adams [counsel for the insurance company] argued that the relevant paragraphs did not amount to a plea of fraud, but I cannot see how an averment that the Appellant was exaggerating his disability "for financial gain" can be anything else."

Later at paragraph 26 another judge of the Court of Appeal referred to "the grossly inflated amount which he received upon the settlement of his fraudulently exaggerated claim".

Interestingly in relation to the issue of re-opening settled QOCS claims due to a subsequent allegation of fundamental dishonesty Practice Direction 44 12.4(b) says:-

"(b)     where the proceedings have been settled, the court will not, save in exceptional circumstances, order that issues arising out of an allegation that the claim was fundamentally dishonest be determined in those proceedings;"

This case is being appealed to the Supreme Court, leave having been granted on 28 July 2015, the case reference is UKSC 2015/0099. As at the time of writing it has not been listed. You can follow the progress of the case at https://www.supremecourt.co.uk/current-cases/index.html or on my blog: Kerry on QOCS: Book, Updates and links.

**In Summers v Fairclough Homes Ltd [2012] UKSC 26**

the Supreme Court held that a court had the power to strike out a claim in its entirety in the event of fraud, but that that power should only be exercised in very exceptional circumstances. It has rarely been used.

Under the principles of this case a claimant would generally receive the genuine element of a claim even if a court found that s/he had dishonestly claimed other losses. This case is in a sense a forerunner of Section 57 of the

Criminal Justice and Courts Act 2015. Here the Supreme Court said, at paragraph 1:-

"The principal issues in this appeal are whether a civil court ("the court") has power to strike out a statement of case as an abuse of process after a trial at which the court has held that the defendant is liable in damages to the claimant in an ascertained sum and, if so, in what circumstances such a power should be exercised."

There was no doubt that the claimant had had an accident which was the defendant's fault but the trial judge found that he had exaggerated his symptoms to the extent of being fraudulent and had deliberately lied to those preparing medical reports.

At paragraph 33 of its judgment the Supreme Court said:-

"33. We have reached the conclusion that, notwithstanding the decision and clear reasoning of the Court of Appeal in Ul-Haq, the court does have jurisdiction to strike out a statement of case under CPR 3.4(2) for abuse of process even after the trial of an action in circumstances where the court has been able to make a proper assessment of both liability and quantum. However, we further conclude, for many of the reasons given by the Court of Appeal, that, as a matter of principle, it should only do so in very exceptional circumstances."

Interestingly at paragraph 45 the Supreme Court said:-

It was submitted that an ascertained claim for damages could only be removed by Parliament and not by the courts. We are unable to accept that submission.

It is for the court, not for Parliament, to protect the court's process. The power to strike out is not a power to punish but to protect the court's process."

Parliament has clearly taken a different view from the Supreme Court in passing Section 57.

Most interestingly of all the Supreme Court considered the role of the European Convention on Human Rights in the context. Specifically the Supreme Court accepted that a judgment is a possession within the meaning of Article 1 Protocol 1 of the European Convention on Human Rights and that the effect of striking out a claim for damages would be to deprive someone of that possession, which would only be permissible if "in the public interest and subject to the conditions provided for by law..."

The Supreme Court said that the State has a wide margin of appreciation in deciding what is in the public interest but that is subject to the principle of proportionality – Pressos Compania Naviera SA v Belgium (1995) 21 EHRR 301 Paras 31 to 39.

"48. It is in the public interest that there should be a power to strike out a statement of case for abuse of process, both under the inherent jurisdiction of the court and under the CPR, but the court accepts the submission that in deciding whether or not to exercise the power the court must examine the circumstances of the case scrupulously in order to ensure that to strike out the claim is a proportionate means of achieving the aim of controlling the process of the court and deciding cases justly."

The court then went on to say, at paragraph 49:-

"The draconian step of striking a claim out is always a last resort, a fortiori where to do so would deprive the claimant of a substantive right to which the court had held that he was entitled after a fair trial. It is very difficult indeed to think of circumstances in which such a conclusion would be proportionate. Such circumstances might, however, include a case where there had been a massive attempt to deceive the court but the award of damages would be very small."

In Akhtar and Khan v Ball, Walsall County Court, Unreported, 10 July 2015, Claim number A23YJ132

the two claimants were found to be fundamentally dishonest and the claims were dismissed, QOCS was dis-applied and the claimants were ordered to pay the defendants £3,000.00 exemplary damages on the defendant's counterclaim for deceit and costs on the indemnity basis.

The court found the claimants to be "complicit in a criminal conspiracy to defraud" Royal and Sun Alliance Insurance plc.

The dismissal of the claims was because they were not made out, rather than under section 57 of the Criminal Justice and Courts Act 2015.

Husband and wife Parveen Akhtar and Mohammed Khan sought damages for personal injury following a road traffic accident when Rebecca Ball, a teacher insured by Royal and Sun Alliance, collided with the rear of a vehicle being driven by Mrs Akhtar.

It was alleged that Mr Khan was a front seat passenger.

The court dismissed both claims, finding that there had been no passenger and that the collision was at such a low speed that it could not have caused the injuries alleged.

The judge added:

"Even if I felt that there had been an accident which had actually caused Mrs Akhtar some injury, I would consider it appropriate to adopt the approach approved as acceptable in some cases by the Supreme Court in *Summers v Fairclough Homes Ltd* [2012] UKSC 26 as permitting a court to dismiss or strike-out an otherwise *bona fide* substantive claim because of the fraud in which that claimant has engaged in the course of the litigation to pursue another false claim." (Paragraph 36).

**Other cases**

In *Gosling v Screwfix and Another, Cambridge County Court,* 29 March 2014, unreported, HHJ Moloney QC found the claimant to be exaggerating both his ongoing pain and the limitations to his mobility following an anthroplasty operation to his knee. This followed a "frankly devastating surveillance video."

In considering whether this amounted to fundamental dishonesty the judge said that:-

"a claimant should not be exposed to costs liability merely because he is shown to have been dishonest as to some collateral matter or perhaps as to some minor, self-contained head of damage. If, on the other hand, the dishonesty went to the root of either the whole claim or a substantial part of his claim, then it appears to me that it would be a fundamentally dishonest claim: a claim which depended as to a substantial or important part of itself upon dishonesty." (Paragraph 45).

The judge rejected the contention that fundamental dishonesty could only be found where "the dishonesty went to the root either of liability as a whole or damages in their entirety." (Paragraph 49).

Here the claimant was found to be fundamentally dishonest as the dishonesty related to a "very substantial element of his claim" both in respect of general damages and damages for future care.

In *Creech v Severn Valley Railway*, 25 March 2015, Telford County Court, unreported, District Judge Rodgers made a finding of fundamental dishonesty and thus denied the claimant the protection of Qualified One-Way Costs Shifting and ordered the claimant to pay defence costs of over £11,000.00.

The claimant was a security guard who fractured his shoulder and brought a personal injury claim on the ground that he had tripped on matting left behind after an ice-rink had been removed from a railway station in Worcester where the defendant company had installed it to entertain families while the railway was closed.

The judge accepted evidence from the defendant company that the ice-rink was still on the concourse at the time that the accident was alleged to have happened and had not been dismantled and therefore the claimant could not have been telling the truth. The judge rejected a suggestion that the claimant had simply made a mistake in his evidence.

In September 2014 District Judge Dudley, sitting at Southend County Court, said that he had "absolutely no doubt whatever in my mind" that the claimant had been fundamentally dishonest in giving evidence and thus he deprived the claimant of the protection of Qualified One-Way Costs Shifting and ordered the claimant to pay costs of £6,000.00 in addition to the £1,000.00 costs of the application by the defendant for a ruling that the claimant had been fundamentally dishonest.

The defendant was insured with Admiral and its insured was accused of driving into the back of the claimant's car after the claimant performed an emergency stop to avoid a collision with a motorbike. The claimant alleged that he had suffered neck and back whiplash injuries which persisted for months and obtained GP reports for himself and his passenger.

The court held that in fact there had been no contact at all between the two vehicles.

In *Alpha Rocks Solicitors v Alade* [2015] EWCA Civ 685

the Court of Appeal overturned a decision of the judge striking out the claim by solicitors to recover their costs; the judge had found that the bills were fraudulently exaggerated and mis-stated.

The strike out was on the basis of an abuse of the process of the court – CPR 3.4(2)(b) under the inherent jurisdiction of the court.

No oral evidence was called and the decision was made on the basis of written evidence and the documents.

The court quoted from *Summers v Fairclough Homes* [2012] 1 WLR 2004 where the Supreme Court approved the decision in *Masood v Zahoor (Practice Note)* [2009] EWCA Civ 650 and where they had refused to strike out, after a trial on quantum, a massively overstated personal injury claim.

Here the Court of Appeal found that the judge had, in spite of repeated warnings to himself, conducted a mini fraud trial without hearing any witnesses. He decided that the solicitor was lying and that other witnesses were untruthful without them being cross-examined. The Court of Appeal found that to be a most unsatisfactory state of affairs.

**Comment**

This, and other similar decisions, suggest that the Court of Appeal and the Supreme Court will not be comfortable with Section 57 of the Criminal Justice and Courts Act 2015 which requires a court to strike the matter out even after judgment has been given in the Claimant's favour if there is fundamental dishonesty.

Paragraph 704(C) of the Code of Conduct of Barristers states that a barrister should not draft a document containing any allegation of fraud "unless he has clear instructions to make such an allegation and has before him reasonably credible material which as it stands establishes a prima facie case of fraud".

In *Medcalf v Mardell* the House of Lords said:-

"...the requirement is not that counsel should necessarily have before him evidence in admissible form but that he should have material of such character as to lead responsible counsel to conclude that serious allegations should properly be based upon it."

It will be interesting to see if guidance is given to counsel on raising fundamental dishonesty, either in the context of section 57 or Qualified One-Way Costs Shifting.

## The Defence View

Defence Lawyer James Heath, of Keoghs, has said that the new rule on Fundamental Dishonesty brings with it "a lot of potential for satellite litigation".

## Procedure under QOCS re Fundamental Dishonesty

Where there is an allegation of fundamental dishonesty the court will normally direct that issues arising out of such an allegation be determined at trial (Practice Direction 12.4(a)) and where the proceedings have been settled the court will not, save in exceptional circumstances, order that issues arising out of an allegation of fundamental dishonesty be determined. (Practice Direction 12.4(b)).

Where the claimant has served a notice of discontinuance the court may nevertheless direct that issues arising out of an allegation of fundamental dishonesty be determined even though the notice has not been set aside pursuant to CPR 38.4. (Practice Direction 12.4(c)).

As night follows day such an order in those circumstances is bound to be on the indemnity basis, rather than the standard basis.

Given Section 57 of the Criminal Justice and Courts Act 2015. It seems very unlikely that under CPR 44.16(1) a court will only dis- apply QOCS where the whole claim is fundamentally dishonest when Parliament has ruled that any case issued after the new Act has come into force only requires any element of the case to be fundamentally dishonest.

Furthermore much of CPR 44.13 to 44.17 is predicated on the Claimant recovering damages. Thus the central QOCS protection is contained in CPR 44.14(1) which reads:-

"(1)    Subject to rules 44.15 and 44.16, orders for costs made against a claimant may be enforced without the permission of the court but only to the extent that the aggregate amount in money terms of such orders does not exceed the aggregate amount in money terms of any orders for damages and interest made in favour of the claimant."

That rule is fraught with inherent and internal logical problems which I deal with elsewhere.

However it envisages that a damages award may have been made in favour of a Claimant. Then if there has been fundamental dishonesty in relation to part of the claim then the whole claim would have been dismissed even under the pre Criminal Justice and Courts Act law.

I am satisfied that even under CPR 44.16 it is sufficient that one claim in one head of damages being fundamentally dishonest can deprive the Claimant of QOCS protection.

However that is not, on the face of it, what CPR 44.16(1) says as it requires "the claim" to be fundamentally dishonest.

The position now appears to be that section 57 applies where the claim would have been won and CPR 44.16 where the claim is lost. Either way any fundamental dishonesty anywhere triggers the adverse consequences of either losing a case that was won or being deprived of QOCS protections in a lost case.

**Advice re Fundamental Dishonesty**

The Judiciary Working Group Guide for Litigants in Person, prepared by six Circuit Judges, states:-

"Too often (indeed far too often) witnesses who have had statements prepared for them by solicitors tell the Judge that matters in the statement are not correct; they say (all too believably) that they simply signed what the solicitor had drafted for them without reading it through carefully and critically."

It is of extreme importance that solicitors check with their clients that they have read and understood every word of their statement.

Careful attendance notes should be made. A separate statement should be signed by the client and kept on file and be along the lines of:-

"I have read and understood my Witness Statement and I have had any parts that I was unsure about explained to me and I confirm that the statement is true and accurate in every regard. I understand that any inaccuracy in my statement may lead to my whole claim being thrown out and me being ordered to pay the other side's costs as well as my own solicitor's costs and disbursements."

**Multi-party cases**

Both QOCS and section 57 apply to multi-party cases in the same way as they do to single party cases.

# Chapter 6

# Pre-Jackson Funding Arrangements

# PRE – JACKSON FUNDING AGREEMENTS

## Pre-Action Disclosure

Pre-action disclosure applications under section 33 of the Senior Courts Act 1981 or section 52 of the County Courts Act 1984 are not protected by QOCS (CPR 44.13(1)).

## Pre 1 April 2013 Conditional Fee Agreements, ATE etc

Put simply, if prior to 1 April 2013 there was in place a claimant conditional fee agreement or collective conditional fee agreement or ATE or membership organisation indemnity, then QOCS protection does not apply.

I can understand why, if ATE insurance or membership organisation protection is in place, QOCS should not apply as it would be unfair for a defendant to pay the recoverable ATE premium to a clamant who, on the face of it, is at no risk of paying costs.

However the success fee is to reward the lawyer for taking the chance of getting no fee because the case is lost. This has nothing to do with the risk of the defendant's costs being payable.

Why should a claimant with a CFA with a success fee, but no ATE, lose QOCS protection? Surely it is in the defendant's interest as well, as they would be off the hook for the ATE premium, the whole point being that it is cheaper for the insurance industry to recover no costs but pay no ATE.

This thinking is as woolly as a mammoth.

CPR 44.17 provides that QOCS "does not apply to proceedings, where the claimant has entered into a pre-commencement funding arrangement (as defined in rule 48.2)".

A pre-commencement funding arrangement is a creature "as defined in rule 48.2" (CPR44.17), so, naturally, one looks at CPR48.2, where at CPR 48.2(1)(a)(i) one will find the following:

"48.2(1) A pre-commencement funding arrangement is-
………..
    (i)      a funding arrangement as defined by rule 43.2(1)(k)(i) where……"

CPR 43.2(1)(k)(i) defines a funding arrangement as "an arrangement where a person has –

(i)     entered into a conditional fee agreement or a collective conditional fee agreement which provides for a success fee within the meaning of Section 58(2) of the Courts and Legal Services Act 1990".

A first day trainee can do better than that.

So QOCS applies to all personal injury proceedings where there is no pre-1 April 2013 claimant recoverable success fee or ATE or membership organisation premium in place.

However, in *Casseldine v The Diocese of Llandaff Board for Social Responsibility (a charity)* Cardiff County Court, 3 July 2015, Claim 3 YU56348

Cardiff County Court held that a claimant enjoyed Qualified One-Way Costs Shifting, and thus protection from paying the successful defendant's costs in a personal injury case, even though the claimant had entered into a pre-1 April 2013 Conditional Fee Agreement (CFA) with recoverable additional liabilities.

That CFA had been terminated by the first solicitors on 30 January 2013 before proceedings were issued. The claimant entered into another CFA on August 2013 with her new solicitors.

DJ Phillips distinguished the case from *Landau v Big Bus Company Ltd* [2014] SCCO on the grounds that here no proceedings had been commenced under the first CFA and as the solicitors had terminated it there was never any entitlement to any success fee or costs.

As the claimant only issued proceedings under the second CFA, entered into post recoverability, the court was never able to order the defendant to pay additional liabilities.

The purpose of the rules was to allow QOCS protection where a defendant no longer faced an additional liability.

The key difference between this case and Landau is that here proceedings had never been issued. That leaves open the question of what the position is where a CFA is terminated *after* proceedings have been issued.

119

There the defendant would also face no additional liability provided that the new CFA was post recoverability. There seems no reason why the issuing of proceedings should affect the central point that QOCS is allowed where a defendant does not face an additional liability.

The judge here did not have to decide that point as he could distinguish Landau. However he did say, correctly:-

"31. In my judgment the case of Landau is distinguishable and in any event even if it were not, and with the greatest of respect to Master Haworth, the decision is not binding upon me."

That suggests that DJ Phillips would have made the same decision even if proceedings had already been issued under the original CFA.

My view is that DJ Phillips is right.


## NIL SUCCESS FEE

Does Qualified One-Way Costs Shifting (QOCS) apply to a case where there is a success fee but that success fee is set at nil?

Such an arrangement was not uncommon; it is widely used in cases where Before the Event legal insurance is in place and was often used where claims were funded by a Trade Union. The issue affects a huge number of agreements.

This scenario is simply not addressed in the rules, possibly because the members were unaware of the existence of such arrangements.

As we have seen above, QOCS does not apply to "proceedings where the claimant has entered into a pre-commencement funding arrangement (as defined in Rule 48.2)". (CPR 44.17).

CPR 48.2 (1) says:-

"(i)       a funding arrangement as defined by rule 43.2(1)(k)(i) where –

(aa)      the agreement was entered into before 1 April 2013 specifically for
         the purposes of the provision to the person by whom the success fee
         is payable of advocacy or litigation services in relation to the matter

120

that is the subject of the proceedings in which the costs order is to be made..."

Clearly a Conditional Fee Agreement with a nil success fee does indeed have a success fee, albeit that that success fee is nil.

However in circumstances where there is no success fee payable, because it is nil, it seems to me that there is no provision to the person "by whom the success fee is payable" of the relevant services so as to come within the definition of "a funding arrangement" so as to disqualify the claimant from the protection of QOCS.

The Oxford English Dictionary defines "payable" as:-

1. that is to be paid; due, owing; falling due

2. that can be paid; capable of being paid

Pay is defined as:-

"The action of paying, as a verb it is defined as:-

1. to give

2. (personal) what is due in discharge of a debt, or as a return for services done, or goods received, or in compensation for injury done; to remunerate, recompense.

3. to give a recompense for, to recompense, reward, requite (a service, work, or action of any kind)

4. to give, deliver, or hand over (money, or some other thing) in return for goods or services, or in discharge of an obligation; to render (a sum or amount owed).

5. to give or hand over the amount of, give money in discharge of (a debt, dues, tribute, tithes, ransom, fees, hire, wages, etc.)

6. to give money or other equivalent in return for something or in discharge for an obligation;"

In my view there cannot be payment of zero and therefore there can be nothing payable and therefore a nil success fee cannot be "payable" and therefore such an arrangement is not disqualified from QOCS protection.

I am reinforced in that view by an entirely different line of reasoning.

CPR 43.2(1)(k)(i) defines a "'funding arrangement' as an arrangement where a person has –

(i) entered into a conditional fee agreement or a collective conditional fee agreement which provides for a success fee within the meaning of section 58(2) of the Courts and Legal Services Act 1990"

Section 58 (2) (b) of the Courts and Legal Services Act 1990 says "a conditional fee agreement provides for a success fee if it provides for the amount of any fees to which it applies to be increased, in specified circumstances, above the amount which would be payable if it were not payable only in specified circumstances."

Given that a 0% success fee does not provide for the amount of any fees to be increased, then such a CFA is not a funding arrangement within 43.2(1)(k)(i) at all; therefore the Claimant has not entered into a pre-commencement funding agreement (subject to any ATE), so QOCS applies.

Thus on balance, my view is that a pre-1 April 2013 Conditional Fee Agreement with a success fee set at nil DOES attract the protection of QOCS.

The courts must give a purposive construction to legislation and secondary legislation and rules approved by Parliament. Clearly the intention was that a party who is not seeking to recover any additional liability from the other side should attract QOCS protection, or to put it another way a person who is seeking to recover an additional liability from the other side should be deprived of QOCS protection.

In those circumstances, where there is nothing in fact recoverable from the other side, the purposive construction would give the claimant QOCS protection.

Note that if there was any recoverable After-the-Event insurance premium that disqualifies the claimant from QOCS protection.

QOCS applies unless there is a pre-commencement funding agreement as defined in CPR 48.2, although it can then be dis-applied in certain circumstances, for example if the claim is struck out on the ground that the claimant has disclosed no reasonable grounds for bringing the proceedings (CPR 44.15(a)).

CPR 48.2 refers back to the definitions in the old CPR 43.2(1) (k)(i – iii) which required only that the Conditional Fee Agreement provided for a success fee, or that the party had taken out an After-the-Event insurance policy.

The definitions at CPR 48.2(1) (aa) and (bb) (ii) now expressly require that the success fee "is payable" or that the party is "seeking to recover" the insurance premium. Either eventuality can only occur if the claimant has won in which case s/he obviously does not need QOCS protection.

These appear to be deliberate qualifications as although the wording is largely taken from section 58(4) of the Courts and Legal Services Act 1990 and section 29 of the Administration of Justice Act 1985 as amended by the Legal, Sentencing and Punishment of Offenders Act 2012, those phrases first appear in April 2013 and are absent from the old definition of "funding arrangement" at CPR 43.2(1)(k)(i).

This produces the absurdity set out above, that is that QOCS is only dis-applied if the claimant has won and does not need it anyway!

The relevance of this absurdity is that it highlights just how badly the Civil Procedure Rules dealing with QOCS have been drafted and reinforces the need for a purposive construction by the courts, that is that QOCS should apply save to the extent and for the periods during which, the case was funded by way of a pre-Jackson funding arrangement whereby the defendant faced paying a recoverable additional liability.

That is essentially the line taken by Cardiff County Court in Casseldine v The Diocese of Llandaff Board for Social Responsibly (a charity) 3 July 2015 but not by the Senior Courts Costs Office in Landau v The Big Bus Company 31 October 2014.

I am grateful to Mark Carlisle in relation to this piece.

**Appeals where recoverable additional liability in relation to original hearing**

In _Landau v The Big Bus Company_, 31 October 2014, Senior Courts Cost Office, Master Haworth, held that where there had been a recoverable additional liability in relation to the trial and a second conditional fee agreement was entered into, without a recoverable additional liability, for the appeal, the claimant did not get the benefit of Qualified One-Way Costs Shifting for the appeal.

Master Haworth held that reference to "proceedings" in the rules means "claim" and that the proceedings, both at first instance and on appeal, plainly concern the same claim:

"It is obvious and was plainly intended that "proceedings" in CPR 44.13(1) and CPR 44.17 includes an appeal."

Here the claimant contended that the claim at first instance and on appeal were different "proceedings" for the purposes of CPR 44.17. Accordingly as he did not have a "pre-commencement funding arrangement" relating to the appeal, CPR 44.17 did not apply and thus QOCS applied.

The defendant submitted that the case did not turn on the construction of "proceedings" as the wording of CPR 48.2 makes that determination unnecessary. In the alternative, the second defendant's case was that the whole case from issue to conclusion, including any appeal, is one "proceedings". Thus a pre-commencement funding arrangement in respect of any part of the proceedings deprives the claimant of QOCS protection in relation to any part of the proceedings.

The Master upheld that submission by the defendant.

This decision has been distinguished in Casseldine v The Diocese of Llandaff Board for Social Responsibility (a charity) Cardiff County Court 3 July 2015, Claim 3YU56348.

Both are first instance decisions of equal weight and are not binding on any other court. Here the judge indicated, obiter, that he thought that Landau may have been wrongly decided. I agree

**Joining new parties post 1 April 2013**

What is the position if, for example, there is a pre-1 April 2013 conditional fee agreement against one defendant but post-1 April 2013 a second defendant is joined?

Clearly QOCS does not apply in relation to the first defendant, but does it apply in relation to the second defendant?

Following *Landau* my view is that these are the same "proceedings" and as the claimant has a pre-commencement funding arrangement in relation to those proceedings s/he cannot get the benefit of QOCS protection in relation to any part of the claim. Adding another party does not create a fresh claim or fresh proceedings.

It may be that the success fee is recoverable against a party joined post 1 April 2013. Assuming that no defendant has been named in the conditional fee agreement – see my blog CFAs: Never Name the Defendant – there is no reason why, if appropriately worded, it should not cover new defendants. After all that is the position if a CFA was entered in to prior to 1 April 2013 but proceedings are not issued until much later.

In Engeham v London & Quadrant Housing Ltd & Academy of Plumbing Ltd, 1 December 2015 the Court of Appeal held that a claimant could recover costs against a defendant even though a defendant with a different name was named in the Conditional Fee Agreement.

There have been various decisions on this point and it is clear that if the defendant is not named then costs and, if appropriate, the success fee can be recovered in the usual way.

The potential problem arises when the defendant is wrongly named.

Here the Court of Appeal held that the definition of "win" in the Conditional Fee Agreement is not restricted to who pays and the meaning of win should be widely construed as "in any way you derive benefit pursuing the claim".

My advice remains that you should not name the defendant.

## Discontinuing and starting again

Suppose the claim in which there was a pre-commencement funding arrangement is discontinued and fresh proceedings brought on the same facts.

The issue would be the same as in the Landau case – that is whether a fresh action on the facts as a previous action where the claimant has entered into a pre-commencement funding arrangement amounts to the same "proceedings".

In my view the court could decide that either way but my inclination is that they would find that they are the same "proceedings" and thus would not grant QOCS protection.

Quite separately the court could view such conduct as an abuse of process and strike the whole new claim out.

All of this demonstrates how poor the wording of CPR 44.13 to 44.17 is. To rewrite the whole costs regime in a couple of pages of A4 is absurd.


## Assignment

Supposing a pre-commencement funding arrangement, a conditional fee agreement, is purportedly assigned but that assignment is held not to be valid and thus a post 1 April 2013 retainer is relied upon.

Does that new retainer attract QOCS protection?

Following _Landau_ I think not. The intricacies of the funding arrangements do not stop it being the same proceedings, the same claim.

If an appeal with a fresh CFA post 1 April 2013 does not attract QOCS protection I cannot see how the same proceedings with a fresh CFA can attract such protection.

However the Casseldine case-see above-gives grounds for arguing overwise.

**CPR 52.9A**

In *JE v Secretary of State for the Home Department* [2014] EWCA Civ 192

the Court of Appeal considered the interplay, or lack of it, between Qualified One-Way Costs Shifting and CPR 52.9A, which reads:-

"Orders to limit the recoverable costs of an appeal
52.9A

(1) In any proceedings in which costs recovery is normally limited or excluded at first instance, an appeal court may make an order that the recoverable costs of an appeal will be limited to the extent which the court specifies.

(2) In making such an order the court will have regard to –

(a) the means of both parties;

(b) all the circumstances of the case; and

(c) the need to facilitate access to justice.

(3) If the appeal raises an issue of principle or practice upon which substantial sums may turn, it may not be appropriate to make an order under paragraph (1).

(4) An application for such an order must be made as soon as practicable and will be determined without a hearing unless the court orders otherwise."

Here the applicant was appealing against an order of the Immigration and Asylum Upper Tribunal and sought an order as follows:-

"(a) That the appellant's reasonable incurred disbursements (court fees) be paid by the Respondent in any event;

(b) that the Respondent be prevented from recovery of costs, save for misconduct, against the appellant in any event; and

(c) that if the appellant is successful in her appeal in full or part the usual costs rules apply."

127

The application was made on 18 February 2014 in relation to an appeal to be heard on 25 February 2014.

The Court of Appeal rejected the application, holding that the rule does not contemplate an order in favour of just one party win or lose, but rather allows the Court of Appeal to replicate the lower court costs regime where the appeal is from a no, or low, costs regime.

Qualified One-Way Costs Shifting is a separate regime governed by separate rules (paragraph 9).

The Court of Appeal then went on to deal with CPR 52.9(A) applications, stressing that they must be made promptly and should usually be made in writing.

"10.    If an appeal is brought from a "no costs" or "low costs" jurisdiction, both parties should give prompt consideration as to whether they (a) want and (b) would qualify for such an order. Very often they will not want such an order, because they desire to recover their costs if they win. So be it.

11.     It is important that any application for an order under rule 52.9A is made at an early stage, so that both parties know the costs regime under which they are proceeding. Rule 52.9A(4) requires the application to be made "as soon as practicable". That does not mean immediately. It envisages that both parties will require a reasonable time in which to consider their position.

12.     If the appellant seeks an order under rule 52.9A, it may be convenient and economic to include such an application in the appellant's notice, but the rule does not require that. Mr Paul Joseph for the Secretary of State points out that both parties may need time to consider their position once they know whether permission to appeal has been granted and upon what grounds. He suggests that a sensible cut-off point would be two weeks after the grant of permission has been notified to the respondent. That is the date by which the respondent must serve the respondent's notice if any. I can see force in that submission but it is not necessary to decide that question in the present case. Furthermore it would be undesirable to attempt to cater for all the factual circumstances which may arise. Anyway, it is not the function of this court to re-write the rules.

13.     Once made the application can then be dealt with in writing at modest cost, unless the court otherwise orders. Any challenge to the court's decision will not be entertained unless the court has made a clear error of principle.

14.     In the present case the applicant has applied far too late for an order which the court has no power to make. I expressly hope that no such application will ever be made again on the eve of an appeal.

15.     It will be helpful if the literature provided by HMCTS to appellants and respondents drew attention to the court's power under rule 52.9(A) and the need to make any application under that rule as soon as practicable. In the meantime I hope that appellants and respondents take note of this judgment."

## RETROSPECTION

As we have seen QOCS applies to all personal injury proceedings, where there is no pre-1 April 2013 claimant recoverable success fee or ATE or membership organization's premium in place.

Thus it is fully retrospective in all other cases, covering cases that have been going on for years, which may come as a shock to insurers. This was confirmed by the Court of Appeal in *Wagenaar v Weekend Travel Limited t/a Ski Weekend and Serradji (Third Party)* [2014] EWCA Civ 1105.

The transitional provision is new CPR 44.17.

"44.17 This Section does not apply to proceedings where the claimant has entered into a pre-commencement funding arrangement (as defined in rule 48.2)".

See above for my analysis of this definition, but, as a pre-commencement funding arrangement can, under CPR 48.2 ONLY be pre-1 April 2013, it follows that any other pre-1 April 2013 arrangement is covered by QOCS, for example legally aided clients.

In *Wagenaar v Weekend Travel Limited t/a Ski Weekend and Serradji (Third Party)* [2014] EWCA Civ 1105 the Court of Appeal said:

"28. Under this ground of appeal, Mr Cannon argued that the effect on the defendant of applying QOCS to this case was unfair and prejudicial and, perhaps more importantly, avoidable. He submitted that the defendant had taken all its litigation decisions before the new rules were even published and that imposing them on the defendant some 6 weeks after their introduction was inappropriate. The rules should not have been retrospective.

29. It is, of course, true that the effect of the introduction of QOCS on the defendant has been unfortunate, since if the matter had been tried 2 months earlier, the costs consequences of the outcome of the litigation would have been quite different. But this unfortunately is an inevitable consequence of procedural reform. There has to be a cutoff point and someone will always be on the cusp of it.

30. In my judgment, however, the legal point is unsound. It is well established that the presumption against retrospection does not apply to legislation concerned with matters of procedure, and that provisions of that nature are to ·be construed as retrospective unless there is a clear indication that that was

not the legislature's intention (see Halsbury's Laws of England, 5th edition, volume 96 at paragraph 1189). There is nothing in CPR Rules 44.13 to 44.17 to indicate that they were not intended to be retrospective. Indeed, they show clearly that they were. The amendments are expressed to take effect on 1st April 2013, and there are transitional provisions in CPR Part 44.17 that apply in particular cases – namely where the claimant has entered into a pre-commencement funding agreement."

On the face of it a claimant without a CFA or ATE with, say, a £200,000 costs order against them prior to 1st April 2013 does not now have to pay. A costs order where the defendant won on liability is worthless. Where the defendant won on a Part 36 offer, then generally the order is only as good as the level of damages recovered by the claimant.

This also highlights one of the odd aspects of the Court of Appeal's decision in *Simmons v Castle* [2012] EWCA Civ 1288 re the 10% general damages uplift to all claimants who prior to 1 April 2013 did not have a Conditional Fee Agreement with recoverable success fee in place.

Such a claimant, for example funded by a before-the-event insurance (BTE) policy, will get 10% extra general damages to compensate them for the non recovery of a non-existent success fee AND will benefit from QOCS to avoid them having to buy adverse costs insurance which in fact they already have through their BTE policy.

Furthermore a defendant gets no Part 36 costs protection until a costs order is made, so late acceptance of a defendant's Part 36 offer does not trigger costs, whereas it did prior to 1 April 2013. So acceptance post 1 April 2013, out of time and the last one, two, three years' costs liability goes, unless you have a CFA with recoverable success fee or you have recoverable ATE.

However I suspect that the defendant will refuse to pay costs unless a set-off for post-Part 36 costs is made, forcing the claimant to go to detailed assessment, except that if the bill is for £75,000 or less it will be a paper-only provisional assessment in the first instance. I hope that no-one in the Court of Appeal is planning any holiday any time soon.

### Retrospective retrospection

Are you free to tear up any agreement providing for the recoverability of an additional liability and thus gain QOCS protection?

The relevant rule is CPR 44.17 which reads:

"This Section does not apply to proceedings where the claimant has entered into a pre-commencement funding arrangement (as defined in rule 48.2)."

New CPR 48.2 is long and complicated but CPR 48.2(1)(a)(i)(aa) – I have not made that up – defines a funding arrangement as itself defined by CPR 43.2(1)(k)(i) – I have not made that up either – as where "the agreement was entered into before 1 April 2013 specifically for the purposes of the provision to the person by whom the success fee is payable of advocacy or litigation services in relation to the matter that is the subject of the proceedings in which the costs order is to be made;

or
…….."

This deals with CFAs, (bb) deals with Collective Conditional Fee Agreements, 48.2(1)(ii) deals with ATE and 48.2(1)(iii) with membership organisation self-insurance.

Any one of these disapplies QOCS. By ending any relevant agreement can you disapply the disapplication and achieve retrospective QOCS protection?

This depends upon the meaning of "has entered into". Clearly the better wording would have been "had entered into" or "has ever entered into" which would have put it beyond doubt. "Has" is not tense specific. "Has my client got a CFA ?" is present tense.

It is clearly arguable either way, but equally clearly the intention of Parliament was to disapply QOCS where recoverability of an additional liability was in place, so on the basis that courts should adopt a purposive construction of legislation, my view is that anyone who has ever had a recoverable liability does not get QOCS protection. That view has been adopted by Master Haworth in _Landau v The Big Bus Company_, 31 October 2014, which I deal with above under "Appeals where additional recoverability in relation to the original trial".

The court took a different view, on its particular facts in the case of _Casseldine v The Diocese of Llandaff Board for Social Responsibility (a charity) Cardiff County Court, 3 July 2015, Claim 3 YU56368_- see above.

However that case does not mean that a court would allow QOCS protection where a party deliberately destroys the pre Jackson funding agreement so as to aquire QOCS.

Even if that worked a court could treat it as an abuse of process and then rule that the case comes within QOCS but disallow QOCS protection by finding an abuse of process.

Don't get me started on CPR 48.2(1)(a)(i)(aa) and its reference to the claimant paying the success fee in a pre-1 April 2013 when the whole point of it all is the abolition of recoverability – the client was not allowed to pay the success fee!

# Chapter 7

# Part 36

# PART 36

## The idea

The basic concept is that the claimant will not be required to pay the defendant's costs if the claim fails, but the defendant must pay the claimant's costs in the usual way if the claim succeeds.

On the face of it this avoids the need for claimant after-the-event insurance and thus dovetails with the abolition of recoverability of the premium from the losing party achieved by section 46 of the Legal Aid, Sentencing and Punishment of Offenders Act 2012 and which applies to insurance policies taken out after 31 March 2013. The theory is that the disadvantage to corporate defence insurers – the "repeat players" - of not recovering costs in the event of victory is outweighed by not having to pay recoverable after-the-event insurance premiums in the event of defeat.

Claimants in personal injury cases could proceed in the certain knowledge that they would never be liable for the defendants' costs; consequently there was no need to take out after-the-event (ATE) insurance; worthless claims would be filtered out by the claimants' solicitors who would not take on useless, and therefore non-fee earning, cases.

In theory this is an excellent idea. We already have no-costs regimes in employment and family work and the Small Claims track is a no-costs zone whatever the type of work. Part 36 is not applicable to any of those areas and is specifically stated not to apply to Small Claims matters.

## The reality

However, the continued existence of the full force of Part 36 of the Civil Procedure Rules in QOCS cases, makes QOCS almost pointless in most cases.

True it is that, subject to various exceptions dealt with elsewhere, a claimant whose claim fails completely will not have to pay the successful defendant's costs, although a full, but generally unenforceable, costs order will be made. This has led Judge Michael Cook to ask

"…under QOCS might even the weakest case now have a nuisance value? Will this be a blackmailer's charter?"

The coach and horses driven through QOCS is the fact that a claimant who *succeeds,* but fails to beat a defendant's Part 36 offer will be ordered to pay all of the defendant's costs from the date of expiry of the time for accepting the offer, although such order is only enforceable without leave of the court up to the level of damages actually awarded by the court.

This is the "damages wipe-out" option, or as Judge Michael Cook puts it

"So, they may lose all their damages in paying costs but will not actually be out of pocket."

The position is simple: no QOCS system can work alongside the continuing existence of Part 36 in such proceedings. The current system in England and Wales implicitly recognizes this; that is why by virtue of CPR 27.2(1)(g) Part 36 specifically does not apply to the non-costs bearing Small Claims Track. Neither is there anything similar to Part 36 in other non-costs bearing areas of law such as family law and Employment Tribunal cases.

One Way Costs Shifting has considerable merit. Qualified One Way Costs Shifting, with Part 36 remaining in full force, is unworkable, with claimants being forced to settle for much less than the claim is worth, or having to fund expensive after-the-event insurance, which avoids the Part 36 problem, but again leads to the claimant losing much of their damages.

Thus an entirely reasonable and honest claimant who wins his or her case but just fails to beat the defendant's Part 36 offer is liable for all of the defendant's costs from the expiry of the date for accepting the Part 36 offer in the usual way.

The only change from the pre-1 April 2013 regime is that the sum of costs paid to the successful defendant cannot generally exceed the amount of damages awarded, although even that is subject to numerous exceptions, most notably that the defendant can set off any shortfall against the claimant's solicitor pre Part 36 costs.

Thus a claimant faces loss of all damages but nothing more, as far as liability to the successful Part 36 defendant is concerned.

However, the claimant will also have his or her own legal costs, or more likely disbursements, to deal with in the absence of any ATE insurance. If a claimant does have such insurance he will have to pay for it himself, as of course the case will have been "won", albeit that it may be a Pyrrhic victory.

Thus in a QOCS case a defendant makes a Part 36 offer. The claimant can accept it or proceed and risk losing all damages AND paying all of his own disbursements from thereon, including counsel's fees, court fees and experts' fees.

It is true that all of these problems exist in all civil work and it could be argued that at least personal injury claimants are off the costs' hook to a certain, albeit limited, extent, in that they pay nothing if the case is lost on liability.

The difficulty is that in virtually all personal injury cases the defendant is an insurance company, and thus has deep pockets. This problem had largely been averted by the widespread availability of after-the-event insurance, whereby the losing claimant never paid the after-the-event insurance premium and the winning claimant recovered the premium from the defendant insurance company.

It is the combination of the abolition of recoverability of the premium, which itself is causing considerable problems in the ATE market, and the continuation of the full rigour of Part 36 which causes the problem.
What goes round comes round.

I am old enough to remember anguished news reports of victims who had won their cases in relation to terrible injuries but received nothing because of an earlier payment to court – the forerunner of Part 36.

# EXERCISE

You act for a claimant in a case where you are reasonably confident, but by no means certain, of winning. You value the damages at £100,000.

    (A)  Under the old regime, with ATE insurance in place to cover own disbursements and adverse costs, including in relation to Part 36, what is the minimum Part 36 offer you would advise the claimant to accept?

    (B)  Does that figure change, and if so what to, in the new regime, with no insurance in place and no counsel on board under a CFA and a claimant who will be unable to pay counsel's fees, court fees and experts' fees in the event of failing to beat the Part 36 offer?

If you act for defendants then state what figure you would expect to be accepted (A) now and (B) under the new regime.

One of the points being missed is the solicitor's risk of being left with a liability for post-Part 36 disbursements that a client who has failed to beat a Part 36 offer cannot, or will not, pay. This is bound to influence solicitor behaviour. There is no point in a client spending a substantial sum on after-the-event insurance to cover this Part 36 risk unless they are likely to recover a sum that exceeds the Part 36 offer by at least as much as the premium, in which case why take out the insurance at all?

Thus the client who beats the Part 36 offer will always question why such expensive ATE insurance was necessary and the client who fails to beat the Part 36 offer will always think that the solicitor should have taken out such insurance.

The initial consideration as to whether to take out unrecoverable ATE insurance essentially to cover the Part 36 risk is not easy.

True One Way Costs Shifting has considerable merit and operates in some states of the United States of America in relation to discrimination claims. Qualified One Way Costs Shifting with Part 36 remaining fully in force in unworkable, forcing claimants, to settle for less than before or to fund expensive after-the-event insurance.

Either way claimants will be left out of pocket, and that is without taking in to account the fact that they will now have to pay some of their own costs, generally a sum equal to 25% of general damages and past special damages, net of Compensation Recovery Unit payments, by way of a success fee.

## CASE STUDY

Robert Males, Managing Partner of Underwoods Solicitors has provided this study of one of our matters .

### Part 36 offers and the effect of ATE insurance

In a recent case the effect of the availability of ATE insurance had a dramatic effect upon whether the client accepted a Part 36 offer made by the Defendant.

The claim was a clinical negligence matter arising out of a hospital infection acquired by an elderly lady when she underwent treatment at the Defendant's hospital. These cases are complicated because there are usually arguments about when and how the Claimant acquired the infection and whether it was due to any breach of duty by the hospital. Causation is another difficult area in these type of cases and there are usually significant arguments by medical experts as to whether any potential breaches of duty actually caused the infection or whether it was due to other factors such as the patient already having the infection when they came into hospital.

In this particular case liability was strongly denied by the hospital and experts were instructed on behalf of both the Claimant and Defendant in microbiology and gastroenterology to deal with issues of liability and causation as well as condition and prognosis. Unfortunately during the course of the litigation the Claimant died and what had been a potentially high value claim mainly due to care costs and adaptations to the Claimant's home disappeared leaving a relatively modest claim.

Counsel was instructed at an early stage in this matter and had given reasonably positive opinions on liability which enabled the Claimant to obtain ATE insurance cover. Counsel advised that the claim was probably worth no more than £10,000.00 although there was some justification for putting forward a Part 36 offer at a slightly higher amount of £13,500.00 and such an offer was made on behalf of the Claimant.

The Defendant responded with a Part 36 offer of £3,500.00 which was initially considered as being too low. It represented approximately 35% of the proper value of the claim and therefore had the Claimant, or in this instance her personal representatives, continued with the claim and been successful they should have comfortably beaten the Defendant's Part 36.

However this was a case with After-The-Event insurance and, as required under the policy, the insurer was advised of the Part 36 offer along with counsel's advice and all of the medical and other relevant evidence. As a result of this the insurer said that the risk was too great and they were invoking a clause under the policy allowing them to withdraw indemnity should the Claimant not accept the Defendant's Part 36 offer.

This put the Claimant and her solicitors in a dilemma. On the one hand the Defendant's offer was clearly inadequate and there was a very good chance it would be beaten at trial if the claim was successful but without insurance had the claim succeeded and the Claimant failed to beat the Part 36 offer then the costs consequences for the Claimant would have been disastrous. The costs of continuing the case through to trial would have run into many tens of thousands of pounds and when faced with the prospect of possibly proceeding and obtaining a few more thousand pounds or the risk of failing to beat the Part 36 offer and facing a costs order of possibly £50,000.00 or more then it was clear to both the Claimant and her solicitors that the risk was not worth taking.

So as a result of the insurer's decision the Part 36 offer made by the Defendant was accepted and as set out above it only represented approximately 35% of the true value of the claim. Had the ATE insurer continued to support the claim then one would have hoped the matter would have succeeded at trial at a figure far nearer to £10,000.00 or a realistic settlement reached at perhaps £6,000.00 or £7,000.00 which would have reflected the litigation risk in the case.

This just shows the very substantial influence that ATE insurance has when considering a Part 36 offer by a Defendant and although the figures in this particular case are relatively low the principles are applicable to any such claim as it is likely that the higher the damages then the higher the level of costs.

141

# Chapter 8

# Discontinuance, Strike-out and Summary Judgment

# DISCONTINUANCE, STRIKE-OUT and SUMMARY JUDGMENT

## Strike-Out and Summary Judgment

CPR 44.15 allows a defendant to enforce "to the full extent of such orders" – that is exceeding damages, *without* permission of the court, where the proceedings have been struck out on the ground that –

(a) the claimant has disclosed no reasonable grounds for bringing the proceedings;

(b) the proceedings are an abuse of the court's process; or

(c) the conduct of –

    (i) the claimant; or

    (ii) a person acting on the claimant's behalf and with the claimant's knowledge of such conduct,

is likely to obstruct the just disposal of the proceedings.

Note that the proceedings must be *struck out* to trigger the costs liability. It is not sufficient that summary judgment has been entered against the claimant. Often an application to strike out and an application for summary judgment are issued and heard together. Prior to 1 April 2013 this may have seemed a distinction without a difference. Now it is hugely important. If a judge awards summary judgment against a claimant as compared with striking out the claim, then the claimant will be protected from an adverse costs order.

Note also that a claimant who is the subject of a striking out application may jump the gun and discontinue the proceedings and avoid liability for costs, subject to the court's discretion to set aside the Notice of Discontinuance, which I shall deal with below.

## Strike out

## No Reasonable grounds

In Wall v British Canoe Union, Birmingham County Court 30 July 2015 a claim brought under the Fatal Accidents Act and Law Reform (Miscellaneous Provisions) Act 1934 was struck out as the claimant had shown no reasonable grounds for bringing the proceedings.

The claimant's husband was killed in a weir whilst canoeing and she brought an action claiming that the British Canoe Union had been negligent in publishing a guide giving a recommended route down the weir whereas earlier guides had recommended portaging the weir.

The defendant successfully argued that there was in law no duty of care and no reasonably arguable claim on causation.

HH Judge Lopez correctly said that in those circumstances Qualified One-Way Costs Shifting did not apply and therefore the costs order against the claimant could be enforced to the full extent without the permission of the court.

In a long and helpful judgment in relation to striking out and summary judgment the judge dealt with Qualified One-Way Costs Shifting at paragraphs 48 to 51.

"48. Rule 44.13(1) CPR provides that the section applies to proceedings which include a claim for damages for personal injuries; under the Fatal Accidents Act 1976; or for the benefit of an estate by virtue of section 1(1) of the Law Reform (Miscellaneous Provisions) Act 1934 arises out of death or personal injury.

49. Rule 44.14(1) provides that subject to, inter alia, rule 44.15, orders for costs made against a claimant may be enforced without the permission of the court but only to the extent that the aggregate amount in money terms of such orders does not exceed the aggregate amount in money terms of any orders for damages and interest made in favour of the claimant.

50. Rule 44.15(1) provides that orders made against the claimant may be enforced to the full extent of such orders without the permission of the court where the proceedings have been struck out on the grounds that (a) the claimant has disclosed no reasonable grounds for bringing the proceedings; (b) the proceedings are an abuse of the court's process; or (c) the conduct of (i) the claimant; or (ii) a person acting on the claimant's behalf and with the claimant's knowledge of such conduct, is likely to obstruct the just disposal of the proceedings.

51. Therefore, where the claimant's claim has been struck out a costs order may be enforced in full. However, in such a case the claimant will not have been awarded any damages so the rule allows full enforcement of the of any costs orders made in the defendant's favour in the proceedings as if the Qualified One-Way Cost shifting did not exist."

## No Reasonable grounds

## Oh What Tangled Webs We Weave

*In Leung v Eftekhari and Eftekhari [2015] Central London County Court, 20 October 2015*

the claim was struck out at a claims management conference and the claimant was ordered to pay the defendant's costs in the usual way but the court also applied CPR 44.15 and thus the claimant lost QOCS protection with the order being enforceable in full and an interim payment of £5,000.00 on account of costs ordered.

The claimant worked for the defendants and lived at their house and alleged that she was bitten by a spider, an allegation repeated in the hospital records. This was an ordinary common or garden spider, not an exotic pet and not a spider that the defendants had introduced into the house.

Unsurprisingly the judge considered that it would not be fair and reasonable to impose upon a householder a duty to keep spiders out of their home and such a duty would be unworkable.

Consequently the judge struck out the matter on the basis that there was no reasonable ground for bringing the claim – CPR 3.4(2) (a). The judge also gave summary judgment to the defendants on the ground that the claimant did not have any real prospect of success (CPR 24.2).

It should be noted that summary judgment of itself never disqualifies QOCS but strike out, essentially on the same grounds, does, but not in all circumstances.

**An Abuse of Process**

**Delay**

In Solland v Clifford Harris and Co [2015] EWHC 3259 (Ch)

a High Court judge upheld the Master's decision to strike out a case on the abuse of process ground where a claimant in a negligence action against solicitors had failed to take any action for 31 months.

The only specific failure to comply with the Civil Procedure Rules was the failure to file an Allocation Questionnaire. That of itself was not an abuse of process and did not warrant striking out, but the delay did.

Strike out on the ground of abuse of process disqualifies a claimant from the protection of Qualified One-Way Costs Shifting.

**Obstructing Just Disposal**

**Failure to attend trial**

In Brahilika v Allianz Insurance plc, unreported, 30 July 2015, Romford County Court

the District Judge found that the claimant's failure to attend the trial of a personal injury action was conduct likely to obstruct the just disposal of the proceedings and thus fell within the CPR 44.15(c) exception to Qualified One-Way Costs Shifting and consequently the defendant was not only granted costs in the usual way but allowed to enforce the full order.

Had the claimant attended and lost the costs order would not have been enforceable.

The judge considered that the just disposal of proceedings involves being able to dispose of them in a way fair to all parties including enabling the defendant to test the claimant's evidence.

Part of the judge's reasoning was that that gave the defendant an opportunity to establish fundamental dishonesty on the part of the claimant. That would cause the claim to be lost in any event under section 57 of the Criminal Justice and Courts Act 2015, but also disqualifies QOCS protection.

**Obstructing Just Disposal**

**Failure to file Pre-Trial Checklist**

In Samantha Woodward v Cardiff Council, Cardiff County Court, 19 August 2015

the defendant made an application to strike out the claimant's claim for failure to file a pre-trial checklist. Before the application was heard the court struck out the claim of its own motion due to that failure and also the non-payment of the trial hearing fee.

The defendant's application to dis-apply Qualified One-Way Costs Shifting was successful with the District Judge finding that the claim was struck out on the CPR 44.15(c) ground that the conduct of the claimant was likely to obstruct the just disposal of the proceedings.

Costs were summarily assessed as claimed with the judge stating that the defendant could enforce the full order without court permission.

The judge based the finding on the fact that the trial was imminent, court time had been wasted and the defendant was continuing to incur additional costs but the claimant was not progressing the claim. That resulted in the just disposal of the proceedings being obstructed.

The case is of interest as the defendant deliberately waited until the claimant's conduct was likely to result in a successful application to strike out and to defeat QOCS.

They had considered an application when the claimant had failed to file a Witness Statement but deliberately waited to see if she would fail to file the pre-trial checklist on the ground that that was much more likely to result in a strike out on one of the grounds that would lead to QOCS being dis-applied.

**Comment**

Defendants are now routinely succeeding in applications to defeat QOCS and are developing a tactical awareness in this field which is not necessarily being picked up by those representing claimants.

## Discontinuance

The general rule is that a discontinuing claimant is automatically liable for the defendant's costs. That rule is disapplied in QOCS cases for the simple reason that a claimant with a weak case would be better off proceeding to trial and losing rather than discontinuing and being automatically liable for costs.

The Practice Direction deals with QOCs and discontinuance. Practice Direction 44 at 12.4(c) provides:-

"(c) Where the claimant has served a Notice of Discontinuance, the court may direct that issues arising out of an allegation that the claim was fundamentally dishonest be determined notwithstanding that the notice has not been set aside pursuant to rule 38.4;"

That clearly envisages that in the absence of an allegation of fundamental dishonesty a Notice of Discontinuance will not of itself trigger a costs liability. Otherwise what is the point of the Practice Direction giving the court the power to determine issues arising out of an allegation of fundamental dishonesty if the power exists anyway?

Otherwise a claimant in such a position who goes to trial and wastes everyone's time and money and loses will generally pay no costs and will be in a better position than a claimant who sees the weakness of the case and discontinues. Clearly with a losing claimant the aggregate amount in money terms of any damages and interest is nil and generally that will be the maximum liability of such a claimant.

This policy point, not in the context of Qualified One-Way Costs Shifting, was recently expressed by the High Court in

*Dar Al Arkan Real Estate Company v Al Refai [2015] EWHC 1793 (Comm)*

where the Commercial Court, a division of the High Court, held that discontinuance had no effect on any interlocutory costs orders.

There the claimant discontinued the action but the defendant was held still to be liable for interlocutory costs orders made in the life of the case. The court pointed out that any other decision would potentially leave a losing claimant who proceeded to trial better off than a discontinuing claimant:-

"As a matter of policy it would be surprising if the CPR provides for harsher consequences on a litigant who discontinues a claim or part of a claim than are typically visited on one who pursues an invalid claim or arid litigation to the bitter end. Surely a litigant who comes to appreciate that there is no point in pursuing a claim or part of one is to be encouraged to discontinue it promptly." (Paragraph 37).

## Discontinuance- Not as simple as you may think

That must be right and presumably is the rationale for a discontinuing personal injury claimant still having the benefit of Qualified One-Way Costs Shifting, that is that it would be absurd to force a potential discontinuer to proceed and lose at trial in order to gain QOCS protection.

However life is not that simple.

In a recent case in Newcastle County Court the claimant had issued against two defendants in a road traffic matter that exited the portal.

The claimants accepted agreed damages of £3,500.00 from the second defendant and discontinued against the first defendant who had never applied to have the action struck out. The first defendant obtained full costs against the claimant with an order that they be enforced in full even though the total exceeded £3,500.00.

Absent CPR 44.15 or CPR 44.16 applying, and clearly they did not in this case, then CPR 44.14 applies. That rule is ambiguous. CPR 44.14(1) allows a costs order made against a claimant to be enforced without the permission of the court up to the extent of damages and interest awarded.

My view is that the Deputy District Judge was wrong in law in allowing enforceability beyond the aggregate of damages and interest.

True it is that CPR 44.14(1) refers to enforcement without the permission of the court, which suggests that there can be enforcement beyond the total of damages and interest with the permission of the court. However if that were the case what is the point of CPR 44.16? It would be otiose as a court would always be able to give permission for the order to be enforced to its full extent by virtue of CPR 44.14(1).

There is a second question as to whether the court, properly exercising its discretion, should have made any award at all. On the face of it CPR 44.14(1) does allow an order to be made and as we have established allows that to be enforced up to the aggregate amount of damages and interest. Thus it could be argued that as an award has been made of £3,500.00, albeit against a different party, that sum can be used to discharge a costs order.

It also raises the policy point which is that if discontinuance of itself triggers costs, as it obviously does in the absence of Qualified One-Way Costs Shifting, then one is better going to trial and losing and wasting everyone's time and money as generally following a lost trial no costs can be enforced against a claimant in the absence of fundamental dishonesty. Clearly if the claimant loses the trial then the aggregate amount in money terms of any orders for damages and interest is nil.

There is a third argument. If one reads CPR 44.14(1) it does not actually say that orders for costs can be made for any amount but only enforced without permission of the court up to the aggregate amount in money terms of any orders for damages and interest. What it in fact says is:-

"…but only to the extent that the aggregate amount in money terms of **such orders** does not exceed the aggregate amount in money terms of any orders for damages and interest made in favour of the claimant." (My italics and bold)

Thus it appears to say that insofar as any order exceeds the amount of damages and interest it cannot be enforced even to the extent of the amount of the damages and interest.

Thus damages are £3,500.00. An order is made for £5,000.00. That order thus exceeds the aggregate amount in money terms etc. and therefore cannot be enforced without the permission of the court.

That is subject to CPR 44.15 and 44.16 which we have already considered. They have no application here.

Thus in my view if a court makes an order for £5,000.00 where the damages etc. are only £3,500.00 then none of it can be enforced without the permission of the court because that is what CPR 44.14(1) literally says.

The problem here is that presumably the court can give permission to enforce the whole sum and that appears to take it out of CPR 44.14, but does not affect the points raised above.

The final non-technical, but probably most important, point is this. The claimant would have been better simply throwing in the towel and losing against both parties, or indeed going to trial and losing as then the client would have received nothing but paid nothing. To win £3,500.00 but then be ordered to pay a greater sum very obviously leaves the client worse off than simply losing completely.

In the absence of fundamental dishonesty that cannot possibly have been the intention of those drafting the rules.

I am not sure how in a non-personal injury claim that is the case in that the losing claimant would have been liable for all of the defendant's costs but would have kept the value of the interlocutory costs orders, a Pyrrhic victory one would think.

However it is most definitely the case in personal injury claims where a claimant could proceed, lose and not be liable for the other side's costs, due to QOCs.

**Jumping the gun**

That raises the issue as to whether a claimant can save the day as far as costs are concerned by discontinuing a claim that would otherwise be struck out, other than where fundamental dishonesty is alleged where the court can consider the matter and award costs where appropriate even if Notice of Discontinuance has been served and not set aside.

Thus an application is made for a strike out on one of the grounds which, if successful, would trigger a full costs order and allow enforcement without the permission of the court as set out in CPR 44.15.

Can the claimant jump the gun and discontinue? Yes, appears to be the answer. Can an advocate at court, faced with the inevitable, discontinue on her or his feet? Can an instructing solicitor write out and serve Notice of Discontinuance while the application is in progress?

Does the court have a general power to set aside a Notice of Discontinuance and thus prevent the claimant from achieving QOCS protection?

Practice Direction 44.12.4(c) allows the court to determine issues of fundamental dishonesty, and thus allow enforcement of a costs order in a QOCS case, notwithstanding that a Notice of Discontinuance has not been set aside.

That does not prevent a court from setting aside the Notice of Discontinuance and proceeding to hear and determine the strike out application when there is no allegation of fundamental dishonesty.

However there is still a potential liability on discontinuance, as QOCS protection does not apply in various situations, e.g. credit hire claims, gratuitous care claims etc. – see below; so I set out the normal rule on discontinuance below.

**Court's discretion to set aside Notice of Discontinuance**

*In Brian Kite v Phoenix Pub Group 2015 Unreported*

the court set aside a Notice of Discontinuance thus allowing the defendant to recover costs on an application to strike out the claim. This flows from the fact that under Qualified One-Way Costs Shifting, Notice of Discontinuance triggers a costs order, but not the ability to enforce that order.

However under CPR 44.15(1) orders for costs made against a claimant may be enforced to the full extent of such orders without the permission of the court where the proceedings have been struck out on certain grounds as specified in that order.

Here the claimant brought a claim for injuries sustained when he fell into an uncovered manhole in the car park of a pub, The Suffolk Punch. The defendant operates a number of pubs in the South West of England and its case was that although The Suffolk Punch had once been operated by it, by the time of the accident it was owned and operated by a different company, Enlighters Ltd which had in fact been dissolved.

The case first came before the court on the defendant's applications to set aside a default judgment entered in the claimant's favor and to strike out the claim. Default judgment had been entered as, following the service of proceedings at The Suffolk Punch, there had been no response. The court set that judgment aside on the basis that there had not been valid service.

152

The judge then considered the defendant's application to strike out and the defendant showed through Companies House and Land Registry records that it had no connection with Enlighters Ltd and was neither the freeholder nor the leaseholder.

The judge agreed to the claimant's application for an adjournment to carry out further investigations.

The claimant produced no further evidence and notified the defendant's solicitors that as the case was covered by Qualified One-Way Costs Shifting they would be unable to recover their costs and in response the defendant's solicitors reminded the claimant of the exception to QOCS where a case was struck out on specified grounds.

Two days before the adjourned strike out hearing the claimant served Notice of Discontinuance, the effect of which would be to deprive the defendant of an enforceable costs order due to QOCS.

The defendant then made an application to set aside that Notice of Discontinuance pursuant to CPR 38.4 so that the strike out application could proceed at the hearing.

At the adjourned strike out hearing the defendant's application to set aside the Notice of Discontinuance was heard first.

The defendant submitted that serving Notice of Discontinuance at such a late stage, following a previously adjourned hearing that had only been adjourned for the claimant to obtain further evidence, was conduct which the court should neither allow nor encourage.

Such tactical maneuvering would produce an unjust result as the defendant would be unable to enforce either the costs occasioned by the adjourned hearing, which had been ordered in their favour in any event, or the costs to which they were entitled following the service of a Notice of Discontinuance.

The claimant argued that they were entitled to service Notice of Discontinuance notwithstanding the consequences that that would have for the defendant under the QOCS regime.

The judge held that a court had an unfettered discretion to set aside a Notice of Discontinuance and in exercising that discretion he had to consider the overriding objective. An important part of that objective was the need to deal with cases fairly and the conduct of the claimant in requesting the adjournment and then serving a late Notice of Discontinuance was unfair.

The judge set aside the notice and allowed the strike out application to proceed and then struck the case out and awarded the defendant its costs of both the application to set aside the Notice of Discontinuance and the application to strike out the claim.

The effect of this was that the defendant was able to enforce all of the costs orders made in the proceedings notwithstanding that it was a case apparently covered by Qualified One-Way Costs Shifting.

**Discontinuance- CPR 38.6**

**CPR 38.6**

"Liability for costs

(1) Unless the court orders otherwise, a claimant who discontinues is liable for the costs which a defendant against whom the claimant discontinues incurred on or before the date on which notice of discontinuance was served on the defendant.

(2) If proceedings are only partly discontinued –

   (a) the claimant is liable under paragraph (1) for costs relating only to part of the proceedings which he is discontinuing; and

   (b) unless the court orders otherwise, the costs which the claimant is liable to pay must not be assessed until the conclusion of the rest of the proceedings

(3) This rule does not apply to claims allocated to the Small Claims track.

(Rule 44.12 provides for the basis of assessment where the right to costs arises on discontinuance and contains provisions where a costs order is deemed to have been made and applying for an order under section 194(3) of the Legal Services Act 2007.)"

## Discontinuance and Fundamental Dishonesty

If the claimant has discontinued in order to avoid a finding of fundamental dishonesty and a consequent costs order, the court may direct that issues arising out of an allegation that the claim was fundamentally dishonest be determined notwithstanding that the notice has not been set aside pursuant to CPR 38.4 – see Practice Direction 12.4 below.

CPR 44.16(1) allows full recovery, that is over and above damages, *with* the permission of the court "where the claim is found on the balance of probabilities to be fundamentally dishonest". See above under "Fundamental Dishonesty" for a discussion of this concept.

In *Clutterbuck and others v HSBC plc and others*, Chancery Division, 2 October 2015

the claimant alleged fraud against one of a large number of defendants and there was a dispute about the form of pleadings.

The day before the application to hear that dispute was due to take place the claimant served Notice of Discontinuance, which usually results in costs to be paid on the standard basis by the discontinuing claimant.

However the court has discretion. Here the judge held that had the fraud allegations failed at trial indemnity costs should have been awarded.

Consequently where a claimant serves Notice of Discontinuance having made allegations of fraud, costs should be awarded on the indemnity, not standard, basis.

## Comment

This was not a Qualified One-Way Costs Shifting case and here it was the claimant alleging fraud. However, given the power of the court in QOCS cases to set aside the Notice of Discontinuance if fundamental dishonesty is alleged by the defendant, it follows that if the defendant is successful in being allowed to enforce the costs order then those costs are likely to be on the indemnity basis.

In any event the court has a discretion to allow a Notice of Discontinuance to be set aside for any reason, but it is the fundamental dishonesty allegation that is likely to trigger indemnity costs.

The irony of this is that discontinuing claimants in QOCS cases risk a higher costs bill than before. In the past a defendant would have been content that the matter was ending and they were getting their costs and indeed would be content with a successful summary judgment application.

Now that Notice of Discontinuance or summary judgment do not of themselves trigger any costs liability on the claimant, defendants are more likely to seek striking out on one of the CPR 44.15 grounds and/or allege fundamental dishonesty so as to obtain an enforceable costs order.

The reason why claimants now risk facing a higher costs order is that the types of claimant behaviour which warrant the defeat of QOCS are also likely to warrant indemnity costs orders.

CPR 44.16(2) also allows full recovery *with* the permission of the court, but now only "to the extent that it considers just". How does this tie in with the concept of "substantial injustice" in section 57, Criminal Justice and Courts Act 2015?

Remember that in both instances the court has had to consider whether to give permission. One sort of hoped that the court would not exercise its discretion to allow enforcement of an unjust order, but that is what Parliament requires it to do under section 57 Criminal Justice and Courts Act 2015. Only *substantial* injustice allows the court to decline to make an order; mere injustice is not enough.

So CPR 44.16(2) allows full recovery with the permission of the court, to the extent that it considers just, where

"(a)     the proceedings include a claim which is made for the financial benefit of a person other than the claimant or a dependent within the meaning of section 1(3) of the Fatal Accidents Act 1976 (other than a claim in respect of the gratuitous provision of care, earnings, paid by an employee or medical expenses);
or
(b)     a claim is made for the benefit of the claimant other than a claim to which this section applies."

I discuss this elsewhere.

CPR 44.16(3) allows the court to make an order against a third party in a 44.16(2)(a) case.

The claimant who loses completely and gets no damages at all and who does not fall within the CPR 44.15 and CPR 44.16 exceptions cannot have any costs order enforced against them. This is the effect of CPR 44.14. This is the only new protection and it protects only complete losers (cases not the people!)

# Chapter 9

# Financial Benefit
# of Another

# FINANCIAL BENEFIT OF ANOTHER

CPR 44.16(2) states:-

"(2)     Orders for costs made against the claimant may be enforced up to the full extent of such orders with the permission of the court, and to the extent that it considers just, where

(a)  the proceedings include a claim which is made for the financial benefit of a person other than the claimant or a dependant within the meaning of section 1(3) of the Fatal Accidents Act 1976 (other than a claim in respect of the gratuitous provision of care, earnings paid by an employer or medical expenses); or

(b)  a claim is made for the benefit of the claimant other than a claim to which this section applies."

The first thing to note is that that provision clearly provides for costs orders to be made against the claimant as well as the financial beneficiary. So a claimant, as well as the financial beneficiary, loses QOCS protection.

CPR 44.16(3) then provides that an order may be made against that other person:-

"(3) Where paragraph (2)(a) applies, the court may, subject to rule 46.2, make an order for costs against a person, other than the claimant, for whose financial benefit the whole or part of the claim was made."

Practice Direction 12.2 then specifically refers to credit hire claims as being a claim for the financial benefit of a person other than the claimant.

 "Examples of claims made for the financial benefit of a person other than the claimant or a dependant within the meaning of section 1(3) of the Fatal Accidents Act 1976 within the meaning of rule 44.16(2) are subrogated claims and claims for credit hire."

That being the case, CPR 44.16(2) and (3) apply, meaning that, with the permission of the court, the order for costs against the claimant may be enforced up to its full extent against the claimant, or an order for costs may be made against the credit hire company.

But it is entirely unclear as to how the drafter of the Practice Direction has concluded that credit hire claims are different from any other type of special damages claim. That is most certainly not the attitude that the courts have taken. The courts have regarded credit hire claims as just another aspect of a claimant's special damages claim. The claimant has had the benefit of the use of the car, and is liable to pay for it, and seeks those expenses from the defendant.

This was put beyond doubt by the Court of Appeal in *Bee v Jenson* [2007] EWCA Civ 923. The logic of that is that any special damages claim opens the beneficiary of the special damages up to a costs order and as we have seen, deprives the claimant of QOCS. I am reinforced in this view by the fact that CPR 44.16(2)(a) – set out above – specifically gives QOCS protection back to gratuitous providers of care, employers who pay earnings and the recipients of medical expenses.

By definition, any item of special damages is, in one sense, for the financial benefit of someone other than the claimant. On the face of it, any special damages claim other than for medical expenses, gratuitous provision of care and earnings paid by an employer, disqualifies a claimant and the recipient of special damages from QOCS.

What are medical expenses? Are care costs medical expenses? If so, why is the exclusion limited to "gratuitous" provision of care? Why not exclude all care costs? What about adaptations to a house? It is hard to see that they can be classed as "medical expenses". Likewise domestic assistance, child minding, home maintenance, decorating, gardening and chauffeuring, for example. The list goes on.

A successful defendant, in a personal injury case, typically an insurance company in reality, will get a full costs order; the issue is enforcement. By definition, the case will be at court, and so a defendant has nothing to lose by seeking in every such case to enforce the order against the claimant and/or the potential financial beneficiaries.

District Judge Gill considered a fixed recoverable costs matter where the claimant was awarded £2,750.00 general damages at trial but failed to beat the defendant's Part 36 offer.

The claimant was awarded costs totalling £3,952.00 up to the date of the expiry of the Part 36 offer.

The defendant was awarded costs from the date of expiry onwards totalling £5,782.00.

During the course of the litigation two other costs orders had been made with the costs being summarily assessed in each case.

The claimant had been awarded £300.00 thus creating a total entitlement to costs of £4,252.00.

The defendant had been awarded £4,492.30 costs giving a total costs entitlement of £10,274.30.

This was a Qualified One-Way Costs Shifting case but the claimant's failure to beat the defendant's Part 36 offer meant that the protection was lost. This enables the full costs order in favour of the defendant to be enforced but only to the extent of money due to the claimant, that is generally a claimant cannot be made to write a cheque.

Here the court started, entirely correctly in my view, by setting off under CPR 44.12 the claimant's entire costs entitlement against the defendant's costs entitlement and this meant that the claimant had no entitlement to costs at all and at this stage the calculation was as follows:

| | |
|---|---|
| Costs due to defendant   - | £10,274.30 |
| Less costs due to claimant - | £4,252.00 |
| Balance - | £6,022.30 |

Then the court applied CPR 44.14(1) allowing the defendant to enforce further up to the extent of the claimant's damages of £2,750.00.

Thus the picture then was:

| | |
|---|---|
| Outstanding balance - | £6,022.30 |
| Less enforcement to the extent of damages - | £2,750.00 |
| Balance outstanding to defendant - | £3,272.30 |

The court declined to allow the defendant to enforce that balance as against the claimant but ordered that the defendant be at liberty to make an application that the outstanding balance of costs be paid by the credit hire organisation – parts of the claim was for credit hire charges – by virtue of CPR 44.16(3) which refers back to CPR 44.16(2).

In my view this decision is entirely correct and the order of deductions is logical, that is that the starting point should be to set off costs due to the defendant against costs due to the claimant.

What remains unclear is as to whether the defendant can set off costs made under the Portal procedure. In my view they can.

A solicitor bringing the case is also a potential financial beneficiary, and is potentially open to have costs awarded against them under CPR 44.16, as well as the general jurisdiction under section 51(3) of the Senior Courts Act, which states:-

"(3)     The court shall have full power to determine by whom and to what extent the costs are to be paid."

In *Excalibur Ventures LLC v Texas Keystone Inc & Ors* [2014] EWHC 3436 (Comm) the High Court said:-

"The discretion is very wide" (paragraph 64).

As far as wasted costs orders are concerned, one of the grounds is that the other party has lost out because of the solicitor's negligent advice to their own client. Thus the argument would run that the claim was weak, proven by the fact that it was lost, and that the defendant has incurred legal costs which, because of QOCS, it is unable to recover from the claimant, and therefore a wasted costs order should be made against the claimant's solicitor.

That is a perfectly feasible argument which is bound to be raised very much more often now. In a pre-LASPO age where a defendant could not only enforce the costs, but actually had a party able to pay in the form of an ATE insurer, there was no point in a defendant seeking a wasted costs order. They are not easy to obtain, but the threat of them is likely to have a chilling effect on claimant lawyers, for obvious reasons.

What about a solicitor's liability under CPR 44.16, as a financial beneficiary, where the hurdle will be very much lower than that of a wasted costs order?

In *Flatman and Germany v Weddall and Barchester Healthcare Ltd* [2013] EWCA Civ 278, the Court of Appeal held that solicitors who help their clients by funding the cost of disbursements on a contingency fee bases, that is without recovering them from the client if the case is lost, should not be liable for costs if the case fails, even if no ATE insurance is in place.

This was a pre-QOCS decision, but the appeal court recognised its importance in relation to QOCS saying:-

"Defendants' insurers can undermine the principle of Qualified One-Way Costs Shifting (which will limit recovery of costs by insurers in failed personal injury actions) by pursuing the solicitors acting for the claimant who fails."

But the Court of Appeal appeared to get a little confused between CPR 44.16 and section 51(3) as it said at paragraph 45:-

"… the legislation does visualise the possibility that a solicitor might fund disbursements and, in that event, it would not be right to conclude that such a solicitor was "the real party" or even "a real party" to the litigation."

That may be true, but that is the section 51(3) test in relation to non-parties orders, included wasted costs orders. It is readily apparent that the test under CPR 44.16 is very different, and the hurdle very much lower. One could be a financial beneficiary of a claim under CPR 44.16 without ever coming near being "the real party" or "a real party".

So the decision in *Flatman*, although welcome, may be seen as of limited application in relation to the test under CPR 44.16. The danger is that solicitors will become over cautious about bringing anything other than the safest claims, and will also be too ready to accept a low Part 36 offer.

I am satisfied that a claim in relation to a minor is not a claim made for the financial benefit of a person other than the claimant. The minor is the claimant, but simply acts through a Litigation Friend, and I am satisfied that QOCS applies to minor claims and that such a claim is not one made on behalf of someone else.

The position is treated as being the same in relation to gratuitous care claims.

Practice Direction paragraph 12.3 states:-

"Gratuitous provision of care" within the meaning of rule 44.16(2)(a) includes the provision of personal services rendered gratuitously by persons such as relatives and friends for things such as personal care, domestic assistance, child minding, home maintenance and decorating, gardening and chauffeuring."

Practice Direction 12.5 reads :-

"The court has power to make an order for costs against a person other than the claimant under section 51(3) of the Senior Courts Act 1981 and rule 46.2. In a case to which rule 44.16(2)(a) applies (claims for the benefit of others) –

(a)   the court will usually order any person other than the claimant for whose financial benefit such a claim was made to pay all the costs of the proceedings or the costs attributable to the issues to which rule 44.16(2)(a) applies, or may exceptionally make such an order permitting the enforcement of such an order for costs against the claimant.

(b)   the court may, as it thinks fair and just, determine the costs attributable to claims for the financial benefit of persons other than the claimant."

Rule 44.16(3) confirms that Rule 46.2 applies to QOCS, that is that before a non-party costs order is made that non party must be added to the proceedings and be given an opportunity to be heard by the court.

Paragraph 12.6 of the Practice Direction makes it clear that such orders can exceed the value of damages awarded.

There is a degree of contradiction between CPR 44.16 and Practice Direction 12.5.

Although the wording of CPR 44.13 to CPR 44.17 plumbs new depths, the general view is that in every QOCS case a full order for costs must be made by the court in the usual way and the issue is then as to the extent to which that order may be enforced.

The language of CPR 44.16(2) confirms that in that it provides for an exception to the general QOCS rule and the order can only be enforced up to the level of damages and interest. What CPR 44.16(2) does is to allow, with the permission of the court, enforcement up to the "full extent" of the order in certain circumstances.

CPR 44.16(3) then enables the court, but does not compel the court, to make an order against another party. So far so good.

However the Practice Direction provides that the order should usually be made against that other person and not the claimant. That is very clearly not what the actual rule says.

I do not see how the drafter of the Practice Direction determines that such orders should only be made "exceptionally" against the claimant and how they should "usually" be paid by the person other than the claimant for whose financial benefit the claim was made.

In practice a defendant should join the credit hire company or other party or whatever and seek enforcement against both.

## Claims on behalf of the estate of a deceased person

The starting point is that claims brought on behalf of the estate of a deceased person in personal injury matters are protected by Qualified One-Way Costs Shifting.

CPR 44.13(2) states:-

"(2) In this Section, 'claimant' means a person bringing a claim to which this Section applies or an estate on behalf of which such a claim is brought, and includes a person making a counterclaim or an additional claim."

It is important to remember that the full costs order is made in the usual way against a losing claimant in a QOCS case and against a claimant who fails to beat a defendant's Part 36 offer.

What QOCS does is to restrict the ability of the receiving party to enforce that order without the permission of the court.

The central restriction contained in CPR 44.14(1) reads as follows:-

"(1) Subject to rules 44.15 and 44.16, orders for costs made against a claimant may be enforced without the permission of the court but only to the extent that the aggregate amount in money terms of such orders does not exceed the aggregate amount in money terms of any orders for damages and interest made in favour of the claimant."

Note that even that restriction is subject to the ability of a defendant to set-off against the claimant's pre Part 36 costs and any surplus owed to them.

Thus let us suppose that damages were £50,000.00 and the defendant's post Part 36 costs were £60,000.00. The defendant can enforce up to £50,000.00 and then has an unsatisfied judgment for £10,000.00. The defendant can set that off against the claimant's pre Part 36 costs, which of course belong to the client and not the solicitor.

CPR 44.15 then gives power to enforce the full extent of any costs order without the permission of the court when the claim has been struck on any of the three grounds listed, that is:-

> "(a) the claimant has disclosed no reasonable grounds for bringing the proceedings;
>
> (b) the proceedings are an abuse of the court's process; or
>
> (c) the conduct of –
>
> > (i) the claimant; or
> >
> > (ii) a person acting on the claimant's behalf and with the claimant's knowledge of such conduct,

is likely to obstruct the just disposal of the proceedings."

CPR 44.16 then deals with circumstances where orders for costs made against the claimant may be enforced to the full extent of such orders, but only with the permission of the court.

The key rule is CPR 44.16(2) which reads:-

"(2) Orders for costs made against the claimant may be enforced up to the full extent of such orders with the permission of the court, and to the extent that it considers just, where –

> (a) the proceedings include a claim which is made for the financial benefit of a person other than the claimant or a dependant within the meaning of section 1(3) of the Fatal Accidents Act 1976 (other than a claim in respect of the gratuitous provision of care, earnings paid by an employer or medical expenses);"

This is most unclear and most unhelpful. However I presume that the executors are the claimants and therefore the claim is not being made for the financial benefit of a person "other than the claimant" even though the ultimate beneficiary of the estate may be someone else.

A different interpretation could be placed on the rule, that is that such a claim is indeed for "the financial benefit of a person other than the claimant" as it will be the children or neighbour or charity or whoever that benefits. However this would have absurd consequences in that if the executors were the beneficiaries, which is obviously common, then the claim would be made for the financial benefit of the claimant and therefore attract QOCS protection but if the executors were not the beneficiaries then it would indeed be "made for the financial benefit of a person other than the claimant".

Thus my instinct is that such a claim does attract Qualified One-Way Costs Shifting protection. In any event this is one of the circumstances in which the court's permission is required to enforce the full extent of the order; it is a discretionary power. Again my instinct is that a court would generally choose not to exercise its power in those circumstances but that cannot be guaranteed.

That is one of the problems with QOCS, which in my view is the very worst of the Jackson Reforms, that is that you will not know until the end of the case, when of course it is too late, whether or not you have QOCS protection.

The Practice Direction in relation to Qualified One-Way Costs Shifting, at 12.2 says this:-

"Examples of claims made for the financial benefit of a person other than the claimant or a dependant within the meaning section 1(3) of the Fatal Accidents Act 1976 within the meaning of rule 44.16(2) are subrogated claims and claims for credit hire."

That is not an exhaustive list but one would have thought that if QOCS protection was meant to be excluded from executors then that example would have been included there as it is a common scenario.

# Chapter 10

# Miscellaneous

## MISCELLANEOUS

**Provisional Assessment**

What happens in the provisional assessment of costs in a matter where the penalty for failing to do at least 20% better at an oral assessment is an order against you for costs of the assessment?

Does this or does this not apply to personal injury cases which enjoy the benefit of QOCS?

**Fixed Recoverable Costs**

Likewise in relation to the escape clause, again requiring a 20% improvement or a punishment in costs.

Incidentally this one-fifth rule dates back as least as far as the Solicitors and Attorney Act 1729.

**Does QOCS Apply To A Claim By a Defendant Against a Third Party?**

No, said the Court of Appeal in *Wagenaar v Weekend Travel Ltd t/A Ski Weekend and Serradj (Third Party)* [2014] EWCA Civ 1105, overturning the decision of the first instance judge.

The Court of Appeal referred to the Jackson Report in which it was stated that the reason behind QOCS "was a way of protecting those who had suffered injuries from the risk of facing adverse costs orders obtained by insured or self-insured parties or well-funded defendants."

The Court of Appeal stated that although the first instance judge was trying to reach a decision that would be fair to the defendant considering that it had been successful in defending the claim, it must be taken into account that the result in relation to costs of joining the CPR 20 claim to the proceedings is what the defendant should have expected, pre QOCS, when joining parties.

The Court of Appeal held that the first instance judge was wrong to hold that QOCS applied to the proceedings between the defendant and the third party and set that order aside.

The Court of Appeal had this to say on this aspect of the case:-

"40. Thus, in my judgment, CPR Rule 44.13 is applying QOCS to a single claim against a defendant or defendants, which includes a claim for damages for personal injuries or the other claims specified in CPR Rule 44.13(1) (b) and (c), but may also have other claims brought by the same claimant within that single claim. Argument has not been addressed to the question of whether QOCS should apply to a subsidiary claim for damages not including damages for personal injuries made by such a claimant against another defendant in the same action as the personal injury claim. I would prefer to leave that question to a case in which it arises. CPR Rule 44.13 is not applying QOCS to the entire action in which any such claim for damages for personal injuries or the other claims specified in CPR Rule 44.13(1)(b) and (c) is made.

41. I am fortified in my view as to the proper construction of the rule implementing the QOCS regime by a consideration of the effect of the judge's construction on some of the more normal cases which I have already mentioned. In medical negligence claims, a claimant may sue a doctor, a health authority and the manufacturer of some piece of medical equipment. It would be strange if there could be no costs orders enforced between the defendants at the end of a long battle in the cross contribution claims between them where it was ultimately proved that the doctor and the health authority were blameless but the injury was caused by a defective piece of medical equipment. In such a case, the claimant's damages might be agreed, and the argument might be almost wholly between the defendants – or possibly third parties, if any of them were not originally sued.

42. In road traffic cases, the typical situation is equally revealing. Injured passengers in a car may sue the driver of the car in which they are injured. That driver may seek to pass on the blame in CPR Part 20 proceedings to any number of other insured parties, such as another driver involved in the collision, or a local authority responsible for maintenance of the road. Again, there might be little argument as to the claimant's entitlement to damages, but significant dispute between the insured parties as to who was to blame. It would be surprising if there could be no effective costs orders made between defendants in their contribution claims (if there was ultimately more than one) and between defendants and the third parties in the additional claims made."

"46. I do not see any reason why the normal provisions of CPR Rule 44.2(2) (a) should not apply in this case as between the defendant and the third party. The defendant chose to join the third party and failed in its third party claim against her. The defendant should pay the third party's costs."

This aspect of the decision raises the issue of whether it is sensible for a defendant to join a third party to an action when the claimant has QOCS protection.

A successful defendant will be unable to recover its costs from the claimant, due to QOCS, but may be liable to the third party in costs.

Consequently a defendant may be better off defending the action and if it loses then bringing an indemnity action against what would have been the third party. This avoids the risk of paying costs to the third party if the defendant *wins*.

An unanswered question is what happens if a defendant succeeds in defending the action and obtains an unenforceable costs order against the claimant – unenforceable because of QOCS. Can the defendant sue a third party for those costs?

**Is QOCS Legal, That Is Is It Intra Vires?**

Yes, held the Court of Appeal in *Wagenaar*.

It said that it is "within the court's full power to determine by whom and to what extent the costs of any proceedings are to be paid under section 51(3) of the SCA 1981" and that that section "is to be read subject to the power of the Rules Committee to make rules of court applicable to particular circumstances concerning the availability of an award of costs, the amount of such costs, and the exercise of the court's discretion in relation to costs."

The Court of Appeal held that the Civil Procedure Rules in relation to Qualified One-Way Costs Shifting contained in CPR 44.13 to CPR 44.17 were rules that the Rules Committee was fully empowered to make.

**Does The Existence Of Defence Junior Counsel's Pre-1 April 2013 Conditional Fee Agreement Mean That QOCS Did Not Apply To It?**

No, said the Court of Appeal in *Wagenaar*. CPR 44.17 provides that the QOCS regime does not apply to proceedings where the *claimant* has entered into a pre-commencement funding arrangement. For QOCS purposes it is irrelevant what the costs and funding arrangement of the defendant are.

171

# Part III

# STATUTES ETC

# Chapter 11

# Statutes etc.

# STATUTES ETC

## Criminal Justice and Courts Act 2015

*Civil proceedings relating to personal injury*

### 57        Personal injury claims: cases of fundamental dishonesty

(1)        This section applies where, in proceedings on a claim for damages in respect of personal injury ("the primary claim")—

(a) the court finds that the claimant is entitled to damages in respect of the claim, but

(b) on an application by the defendant for the dismissal of the claim under this section, the court is satisfied on the balance of probabilities that the claimant has been fundamentally dishonest in relation to the primary claim or a related claim.

(2)        The court must dismiss the primary claim, unless it is satisfied that the claimant would suffer substantial injustice if the claim were dismissed.

(3)        The duty under subsection (2) includes the dismissal of any element of the primary claim in respect of which the claimant has not been dishonest.

(4)        The court's order dismissing the claim must record the amount of damages that the court would have awarded to the claimant in respect of the primary claim but for the dismissal of the claim.

(5)        When assessing costs in the proceedings, a court which dismisses a claim under this section must deduct the amount recorded in accordance with subsection (4) from the amount which it would otherwise order the claimant to pay in respect of costs incurred by the defendant.

(6)     If a claim is dismissed under this section, subsection (7) applies to—

(a)     any subsequent criminal proceedings against the claimant in respect of the fundamental dishonesty mentioned in subsection (1)(b), and

(b)     any subsequent proceedings for contempt of court against the claimant in respect of that dishonesty.

(7)     If the court in those proceedings finds the claimant guilty of an offence or of contempt of court, it must have regard to the dismissal of the primary claim under this section when sentencing the claimant or otherwise disposing of the proceedings.

(8)     In this section—

"claim" includes a counter-claim and, accordingly, "claimant" includes a counter-claimant and "defendant" includes a defendant to a counter-claim;

"personal injury" includes any disease and any other impairment of a person's physical or mental condition;

"related claim" means a claim for damages in respect of personal injury which is made—

(a)   in connection with the same incident or series of incidents in connection with which the primary claim is made, and

(b)   by a person other than the person who made the primary claim.

(9)     This section does not apply to proceedings started by the issue of a claim form before the day on which this section comes into force.

## II QUALIFIED ONE-WAY COSTS SHIFTING

### 44.13

(1) This Section applies to proceedings which include a claim for damages –

    (a) for personal injuries;

    (b) under the Fatal Accidents Act 1976; or

    (c) which arises out of death or personal injury and survives for the benefit of an estate by virtue of section 1(1) of the Law Reform (Miscellaneous Provisions) Act 1934,

but does not apply to applications pursuant to section 33 of the Senior Courts Act 1981 or section 52 of the County Courts Act 1984 (applications for pre-action disclosure), or where rule 44.17 applies.

(2) In this Section, 'claimant' means a person bringing a claim to which this Section applies or an estate on behalf of which such a claim is brought, and includes a person making a counterclaim or an additional claim.

### Effect of qualified one-way costs shifting

### 44.14

(1) Subject to rules 44.15 and 44.16, orders for costs made against a claimant may be enforced without the permission of the court but only to the extent that the aggregate amount in money terms of such orders does not exceed the aggregate amount in money terms of any orders for damages and interest made in favour of the claimant.

(2) Orders for costs made against a claimant may only be enforced after the proceedings have been concluded and the costs have been assessed or agreed.

(3) An order for costs which is enforced only to the extent permitted by paragraph (1) shall not be treated as an unsatisfied or outstanding judgment for the purposes of any court record.

### Exceptions to qualified one-way costs shifting where permission not required

**44.15**

Orders for costs made against the claimant may be enforced to the full extent of such orders without the permission of the court where the proceedings have been struck out on the grounds that –

(a) the claimant has disclosed no reasonable grounds for bringing the proceedings;

(b) the proceedings are an abuse of the court's process; or

(c) the conduct of –

    (i)    the claimant; or

    (ii)    a person acting on the claimant's behalf and with the claimant's knowledge of such conduct,

is likely to obstruct the just disposal of the proceedings.

### Exceptions to qualified one-way costs shifting where permission required

**44.16**

(1) Orders for costs made against the claimant may be enforced to the full extent of such orders with the permission of the court where the claim is found on the balance of probabilities to be fundamentally dishonest.

(2) Orders for costs made against the claimant may be enforced up to the full extent of such orders with the permission of the court, and to the extent that it considers just, where –

(a) the proceedings include a claim which is made for the financial benefit of a person other than the claimant or a dependant within the meaning of section 1(3) of the <u>Fatal Accidents Act 1976</u> (other than a claim in respect of the gratuitous provision of care, earnings paid by an employer or medical expenses); or

(b) a claim is made for the benefit of the claimant other than a claim to which this Section applies.

(3) Where paragraph (2)(a) applies, the court may, subject to rule 46.2, make an order for costs against a person, other than the claimant, for whose financial benefit the whole or part of the claim was made.

## Transitional provision

**44.17**

This Section does not apply to proceedings where the claimant has entered into a pre-commencement funding arrangement (as defined in rule 48.2).

**Practice Direction 44**

## SECTION II – QUALIFIED ONE-WAY COSTS SHIFTING

### Qualified one-way costs shifting

**12.1**

This subsection applies to proceedings to which Section II of Part 44 applies.

**12.2**

Examples of claims made for the financial benefit of a person other than the claimant or a dependant within the meaning of section 1(3) of the Fatal Accidents Act 1976 within the meaning of rule 44.16(2) are subrogated claims and claims for credit hire.

**12.3**

'Gratuitous provision of care' within the meaning of rule 44.16(2)(a) includes the provision of personal services rendered gratuitously by persons such as relatives and friends for things such as personal care, domestic assistance, childminding, home maintenance and decorating, gardening and chauffeuring.

**12.4**

In a case to which rule 44.16(1) applies (fundamentally dishonest claims) –

(a)  the court will normally direct that issues arising out of an allegation that the claim is fundamentally dishonest be determined at the trial;

(b)  where the proceedings have been settled, the court will not, save in exceptional circumstances, order that issues arising out of an allegation that the claim was fundamentally dishonest be determined in those proceedings;

(c)  where the claimant has served a notice of discontinuance, the court may direct that issues arising out of an allegation that the claim was fundamentally dishonest be determined notwithstanding that the notice has not been set aside pursuant to rule 38.4;

(d) the court may, as it thinks fair and just, determine the costs attributable to the claim having been found to be fundamentally dishonest.

## 12.5

The court has power to make an order for costs against a person other than the claimant under section 51(3) of the Senior Courts Act 1981 and rule 46.2. In a case to which rule 44.16(2)(a) applies (claims for the benefit of others) –

(a) the court will usually order any person other than the claimant for whose financial benefit such a claim was made to pay all the costs of the proceedings or the costs attributable to the issues to which rule 44.16(2)(a) applies, or may exceptionally make such an order permitting the enforcement of such an order for costs against the claimant.

(b) the court may, as it thinks fair and just, determine the costs attributable to claims for the financial benefit of persons other than the claimant.

## 12.6

In proceedings to which rule 44.16 applies, the court will normally order the claimant or, as the case may be, the person for whose benefit a claim was made to pay costs notwithstanding that the aggregate amount in money terms of such orders exceeds the aggregate amount in money terms of any orders for damages, interest and costs made in favour of the claimant.

## 12.7

Assessments of costs may be on a standard or indemnity basis and may be subject to a summary or detailed assessment.

# Part IV

# EXTENDING QUALIFIED ONE-WAY COSTS SHIFTING

# Chapter 12

# Extending Qualified One-Way Costs Shifting

# EXTENDING QUALIFIED ONE WAY COSTS SHIFTING

Qualified One Way Costs Shifting applies to all personal injury work without exception, but to no other work at present.

It is proposed that QOCS be extended to defamation and privacy claims – see Ministry of Justice consultation paper – <u>Costs protection in defamation and privacy claims: – the Government's proposals</u> – 13 September 2013. The consultation ended on 8 November 2013 and the Government said, at paragraph 15:

"We plan to publish a consultation response document by April 2014".

That has not yet happened as at March 2016. No explanation has been given but privately there is an acceptance that Qualified One Way Costs Shifting is far more complicated than Lord Justice Jackson thought.

The Government website as at January 2016 simply states "we are analysing your feedback".

In December 2015 the Ministry of Justice announced that recoverability of success fees and after the event insurance premiums in insolvency matters would cease in April 2016.

No such announcement was made in relation to defamation and privacy cases. Very obviously recovery would end at the same time as its introduction of QOCS, just as it did in personal injury matters.

Thus it is unlikely that QOCS will come in defamation and privacy cases until April 2017.

The proposed scheme is on a very different basis to the personal injury scheme in at least five respects:

- it applies to defendants as well as claimants;

- it is means tested;

- protection may be partial or full or nil;

- a party can move in and out of protection and/or have the nature of the protection changed as the case proceeds;

- the "interests of justice" must be considered in relation to non-individual claimants and in relation to all defendants.

Try costs budgeting that.

The idea is that QOCS will be introduced at the same time as recoverability of the success fee and after-the-event insurance premiums are scrapped in defamation and privacy cases, as happened in personal injury work. As at March 2016 no date has been set for the abolition of recovery.

The consultation paper states:

"It is important to note that protecting one side's cost exposure deprives the other of costs to which they would otherwise be entitled, so a careful balance has to be drawn". (Paragraph 10).

Indeed a QOCS system that can apply to both parties in the same case will in some instances be a no costs system, which if successful may herald a full-scale move to the abolition of costs following the event across the English legal system.

Interestingly the consultation paper recognizes that Part 36 retaining its full effect which, together with the Offer of Amends process contained in sections 2 to 4 of the Defamation Act 1996 "should mean that costs protection is lost going forward if the claimant insists on taking the case to trial".

This is also true of personal injury work but was not flagged up by the Ministry of Justice or Jackson as a problem. The language is revealing….. "if the claimant insists on taking the case to trial".

Thus what has for centuries been regarded as the inalienable right of English people is now regarded as tantamount to unreasonable behaviour warranting a costs order. Sometimes, believe it or not, it is the defendant who forces a claimant to trial.

As with personal injury work the pressure will be on claimants to under-settle.

Helpfully the consultation paper contains draft civil procedure rules which would become new CPR 44.19 to 44.28 (Annex B to the consultation paper).

References below are to those draft civil procedure rules. It is proposed that these draft rules form a new Section IV at the end of Part 44 of the CPR.

## Scope

The scope of the proceedings is as set out in the Conditional Fee Agreement Order 2013, SI 2013 No 689, and is repeated in Draft CPR 44.19 which provides that:

"publication and privacy proceedings" means any proceedings which include a claim for a remedy in respect of -

    (a)  defamation;
    (b)  malicious falsehood;
    (c)  breach of confidence involving publication to the general public;
    (d)  misuse of private information; or
    (e)  harassment, where the defendant is a person who publishes a newspaper, magazine or website containing news or information about or comment on current affairs".

If there is a mixed claim involving proceedings which do not fall within that definition then the costs protection only applies to the costs of those proceedings which do fall within the definition. (Draft CPR 44.20(2)).

It remains to be seen whether trial judges will have to have an array of stopwatches so as to state which part of which question in cross-examination related to something within The Definition.

Try costs budgeting that. Presumably the several days of each Costs Management Conference will themselves have to be split into those involved or not involved with proceedings within The Definition.

Section 40 of the Crime and Courts Act 2013 takes precedence over any consideration of an application for costs protection. Section 40 provides for increased costs to be paid by publishers who choose not to join the new self-regulator. The consultation paper says that "in practice this would only affect less well-resourced defendant publishers which chose not to join the new self-regulator, but which sought costs protection". (Footnote 13).

It should be noted that almost everyone with a website is a "news publisher" within The Definition. All that is required is that the website contains news or information about or comment on current affairs. Have a look at any website and you will see what I mean.

Costs protection is available to both claimants and defendants, potentially in the same case.

Draft CPR 44.20(3) provides that at any stage of the proceedings any party may apply for a costs protection order and/or an order setting aside or varying a costs protection order made in favour of another party.

## Procedure

A party seeking costs protection must apply to court for it and must notify the other side.

There are three financial categories, whether this be claimant or defendant, individual or non-individual:

(i)      those of modest means, who should be entitled to costs protection in full ("nil net liability");

(ii)     the mid group of those of some means who could pay something, but not the costs in full, who should be entitled to costs protection in part ("capped liability");

(iii)    those of substantial means, who should not get any costs protection because they would not face "severe financial hardship" if they were ordered to pay the other side's costs.

The consultation paper at Paragraph 27 states that individual claimants who are not of substantial means, presumably categories (i) and (ii) above, "would be entitled to costs protection unless the court was satisfied that they would not suffer severe financial hardship, however they would have to apply formally to confirm this". ( See Draft CPR 44.22(3)).

Thus it seems that there is a double test, a lack of substantial means *and* "severe financial hardship" whatever that means.

It is not clear what the individual claimant has to apply formally to confirm — is it lack of means or the risk of severe financial hardship or both?

All defendants, individual or otherwise, and non-individual claimants, such as businesses or charities, may apply for costs protection.

## Retrospection

Any order for costs protection may provide that the order shall have retrospective effect. (Draft CPR 44.22(2)). Thus a successful party may retrospectively be deprived of costs; that is a party working on the basis that it will recover costs if successful may find out that that is not the case.

## Agreement

The parties are free to agree the costs protection position. The consultation paper gives the example of a national newspaper agreeing at an early stage that the claimant suing it should have full costs protection. Some of us consider that scenario a tad unlikely in practice.

## Statement of Assets

If agreement is not reached, which it very rarely will be, then the matter is to be determined by the judge based on the applicant's statement of assets. The applicant could be a claimant or defendant, and both parties in the same case could be applicants. The statement of assets must be verified with a statement of truth, and must be sufficiently detailed. (Draft CPR 44.26(2)).

However with all parties other than individual claimants there is a further test, namely that "it was in the interests of justice for costs protection to be granted". (Draft CPR 44.22(1)(b)).

Thus an individual claimant must show:

-   modest means; (undefined) and
-   severe financial hardship (undefined) if they had to pay the other side's costs.

Any defendant, as well as the non-individual claimant, has to satisfy those two tests and show that it is in the interest of justice (undefined) that protection be given.

## Severe financial hardship

At paragraph 29 the paper states:

"This test is drawn from the test in relation to costs protection which has existed for some time in legal aid proceedings".

There is then a footnote to that paragraph:

"The current version of the legal aid test is set out in the Civil Legal Aid (Costs) Regulations 2013; that now has a test of "financial hardship". However, the case law (*LSC v F, A and V* [2011] EWHC 899 (QB)) suggest that, while that test might be suitable for legal aid purposes (where the balance is between private individuals and the state), a better test for defamation in order to exclude the very wealthy might be "severe financial hardship" – which was the legal aid test until the rule was changed in 2000. While those considered by ordinary standards to be very wealthy might nevertheless suffer some financial hardship if they had to pay a costs order in full, they could not be said to suffer severe financial hardship".

I am none the wiser.

Draft CPR 44.26 deals with the procedure for assessment of severe financial hardship.

## Means

### Modest means – full costs protection – nil net liability (Draft CPR 44.22)

Such a group would have personal injury style QOCS protection with enforcement of any costs order, for example in relation to post Part 36 costs, limited to damages awarded.

The same issues re set-off and incursion in to pre Part 36 costs apply as in personal injury (see Set-Off).

### Mid group of some means – partial costs protection – capped liability (Draft CPR 44.23)

This group is expected to pay something as they will be able to do so "without seriously affecting their overall financial position". "While they might not be able to pay all of the opponents' costs – and would suffer severe financial hardship if they did so – they could nevertheless pay a reasonable amount".

This sum – a cap of a reasonable amount – would be determined by the judge at the first judicial hearing and will be based on the applicant's statement of assets AND the other side's costs budget.

This raises the fascinating prospect of deliberately preparing a budget designed to fall just short of triggering costs protection.

As one party's costs protection is another party's costs reduction the court must take into account the other side's assets.

The consultation paper, with no hint or irony, states:

"32.    It is important that claimants or defendants who will be liable to pay something towards the costs should know as early as possible what their likely liability would be so that they can make properly informed choices in the litigation".

**Reasonable Amount**

As to "a reasonable amount" there is perhaps history's most unhelpful footnote:

""A reasonable amount" was suggested by Lord Justice Jackson: Final Report, Chapter 19, paragraph 4.7, p 190".

In fairness I think that the author given the task of preparing the paper is being deliberately ironic there.

Draft CPR 44.23(2) ends with "Criteria for determining level of liability", followed by:

"DRAFTING NOTE: The question arises of the criteria to which the court should have regard in determining what would be a reasonable sum for the party to pay. It is proposed that these should be set out in a separate rule rather than listed here (partly to avoid duplication because they are relevant for rule 44.25 also)".

## Substantial means – no costs protection

These are those who "can readily afford to pay the other side's costs", and thus any application by them will be defeated by the "severe financial hardship" test.

"This provision is intended to apply even if a national newspaper, for example, reports that it is losing money; the fact that it continues to run and pay for a substantial organisation should mean that it can afford to pay a claimant's costs without facing severe financial hardship". (Paragraph 37)

## Confidentiality (Draft CPR 44.26(3))

It is proposed that the statement of assets of a party applying for costs protection will be confidential to the court and judge, unless the judge directs otherwise.

The judge will be able to give such directions as she or he thinks fit, for example as to the disclosure of the identity and assets of any party who is not a party to the proceedings but who nevertheless has a financial interest in the proceedings, or in relation to further evidence that might be required.

## Variation or loss of costs protection (Draft CPR 44.21, 44.24 and 44.25)

The parties are free to vary the costs protection awarded. Either party can apply for the Order to be varied. The consultation paper gives potential reasons why a costs protection order should be varied, for example a substantial change in the means of a party with costs protection or a reasonable offer being made, that means that there is no real merit in the litigation proceeding.

Thus a party can make a Part 36 offer and then seek the removal of the other party's costs protection. Whatever the outcome of that application the party is of course free to withdraw the Part 36 offer after 21 days, unless it is accepted within that time, or under the new Part 36 effective April 2015 to time limit the Part 36 offer.

Draft CPR 44.24 deals with removal of full costs protection. Such protection may be removed altogether or replaced by a capped liability. Draft CPR 44.25 deals with capped costs liability orders; these may be resolved, or varied to provide for a different cap.

Variation orders made under those provisions will not be retrospective. (Draft CPR 44.24(3), 44.25(2))

## Retrospective Orders (Draft CPR 44.27)

It is proposed that costs protection be lost with retrospective effect if the party with the benefit of the order:

- has made a claim which has been found, on the balance of probabilities, to be fundamentally dishonest; (Draft CPR 44.27(a))or

- has disclosed no reasonable grounds for bringing the proceedings; (44.27(b))or

- has abused the court's process; (44.27(c))or

- has obstructed or attempted to obstruct the just disposal of proceedings. (44.27(d))

An order granting costs protection may be retrospective (Draft CPR 44.22(2)).

## Enforcement

It is proposed that orders for costs made against a party with costs protection may only be enforced at the end of the proceedings, once the costs have been assessed or agreed. (Draft CPR 44.28(1)).

Thus the non-protected party cannot put pressure on the protected party by enforcing interim costs orders as the case proceeds.

As with personal injury an order for costs enforced only to the extent permitted by a costs protection order shall not be treated as an unsatisfied or outstanding judgment for the purposes of any court record. Draft CPR 44.28(2)).

Again, as with personal injury, a credit reference agency may view matters differently.

## Costs of Applications

The consultation paper hopes that as many costs protection applications as possible can be dealt with on paper but recognizes that oral hearings may be necessary in certain cases.

Costs of such hearings will be in the court's discretion, with a suggestion that the default position be that each party bear its own costs unless the court considers it appropriate to make a different order.

However, in stark contrast to that suggestion, the consultation paper also says:

"A disincentive to satellite litigation on costs protection might be provided by a presumption that a party who unsuccessfully opposes another party's application for costs protection would have to pay the costs of the applicant party on the indemnity basis".

That suggests that any potential applicant might as well have a go.

It is also misconceived to think of costs orders as essentially satellite litigation as often the total of costs exceeds the total of damages at stake. If a potentially successful party is to be deprived of the chance to recover its costs from the other side, then obviously it will have to pay those costs itself. That is a very serious matter indeed and to try and have that decision reached by a rough and ready paper exercise, with a threat of indemnity costs for opposing the application, is wrong.


## Extending the scheme

At paragraph 41 of the paper it says:

"The Government is not seeking views on a further extension of costs protection to other categories of litigation at this stage, but would welcome any comments on the drafting of the rules, and whether they could be simplified or regularised in the event that it is extended further in the future".

That is inherently contradictory but the main point to note is that the Government clearly is considering extending the concept to other categories of litigation.

## The Draft Civil Procedure Rules

Draft new Civil Procedure Rules appear at Annex B to the consultation paper.

Throughout this piece I have indicated the relevant draft Rule.

Draft CPR 44.19(2)(a) confirms that, as with personal injury, it is enforceability, not the making of a costs order itself which is restricted:

"a "costs protection order" means an order limiting the extent to which an order for costs made against the party in whose favour the order has been made may be enforced".

Draft CPR 44.20(3) provides:

"(3)    At any stage of the proceedings –

(a)  any party may apply for a costs protection order;
(b)  any party may apply for an order setting aside or varying a costs protection order made in favour of another party".

Although it does not say so, presumably a party with the benefit of a capped costs order is free to apply to have that varied to make it a full costs protection order; on the face of it CPR 44.20(3)(a) and (b) do not allow the beneficiary of an order, as opposed to the other party, to apply for a variation.

Draft CPR 44.20(1) provides:

"A costs protection order may provide –

(a)  that any orders for costs made against the party in whose favour the order has been made may be enforced only to the extent that the aggregate amount in money terms of such orders for costs does not exceed the aggregate amount in money terms of any orders for damages and interest made in favour of that party; or

(b)  that the liability of the party in whose favour the order has been made to pay the costs of the other party or parties shall not exceed such sum as is specified in the order (whether or not that sum exceeds the aggregate amount in money terms of any orders for damages and interest made in favour of that party)".

Thus, as with personal injury, the limit is on *enforcement*, not in the making of the order, and this is the effect of draft CPR 44.20(1)(a), and the court can limit enforceability to the total of damages and interest awarded to the party enjoying protection. Thus a party enjoying protection is awarded £50,000 damages and interest but has failed to beat a defendant's Part 36 offer; the court may limit enforcement to £50,000, or indeed less.

Draft CPR 44.20(1)(b) allows the court to limit the adverse costs liability to the sum ordered in the cap, whether or not that sum exceeds the total of damages and interest ordered.

Thus a party's liability for adverse costs is capped at £60,000 and they are awarded £50,000 but the losing party has post Part 36 costs of £70,000 where the claimant has failed to beat the Part 36 offer.

The court can order the full amount, but only enforceable up to £50,000 maximum, or order a maximum of £60,000 enforceable in full.

Although a costs protection order may be retrospective the setting aside of such an order cannot be retrospective (Draft CPR 44.24(3)) unless draft CPR 44.27 applies.

The court may make an order setting aside a damages-limited order (Draft CPR 44.20(1)(a) where the court is satisfied that –

(a) that party would not suffer severe financial hardship without the benefit of a costs protection order in the event that (sic) party were ordered to pay costs of the proceedings of another party; and

(b) it is in the interests of justice to make such an order, for example in the light of any offers made to that party.

Where the court sets aside such an order it may substitute a CPR 44.20(1)(b) order, that is a capped liability order unrelated to damages.

The court may vary or revoke a CPR 44.20(1)(b) capped liability order by

(a) revoking the order if it is satisfied that it is no longer reasonable for there to be a restriction on the liability of the party in whose favour the order was made to pay any other party's costs; (Draft CPR 44.25(1)(a)) or

(b) by changing the sum that the liability is capped at. (Draft CPR 44.25(1)(b)).

Such a variation shall not have retrospective effect unless Draft CPR 44.27 is satisfied.

Draft CPR 44.27 lists the circumstances in which protection may be removed retrospectively.

"44.27 The court may make an order setting aside a costs protection order with retrospective effect where it determines that the party who has the benefit of such an order –

(a) has made a claim which has been found, on the balance of probabilities, to be fundamentally dishonest;

(b) has disclosed no reasonable grounds for bringing the proceedings;

(c) has abused the court's process; or

(d) has obstructed or attempted to obstruct the just disposal of the proceedings".

Thus any one of these four conditions being satisfied may lead to the retrospective removal or variation of costs protection.

Crucially the criteria for determining the level of liability generally have not been decided. The consultation paper says

**"Criteria for determining level of liability.**

[This rule, when drafted, might be placed after rule 44.26]".

Likewise there is no assistance in relation to what "severe financial hardship" is or what is a "reasonable" sum to cap liability at.

The process for assessing severe financial hardship is set out in draft CPR 44.26:

"44.26.—(1)     Unless otherwise ordered or agreed by the parties—

(a) a party making an application under rule 44.20(3)(a) must file a statement of assets with the application notice;

(b) where a party makes an application under rule 44.20(3)(b), the respondent must file a statement of assets within 28 days of service of the application notice.

(2) A statement of assets must be verified with a statement of truth and must set out in sufficient detail for the purpose of assessing severe financial hardship the assets of the party making the statement, including but not limited to details of income and capital wherever they may be and any insurance that may be relevant to the question of costs.

(3) The court will not disclose a statement of assets to any other party without a hearing or the consent of the party making it.

(4) The statement of assets will be referred to a judge who will give directions—

(a) as to the disclosure of the identity and assets of any person who is not a party to the proceedings but who has a financial interest in the proceedings;

(b) as to any further evidence that may be required for the purpose of assessing severe financial hardship;

(c) as to whether the statement of assets and any such further evidence are to be shown to any other party and, if so, whether subject to restrictions as to their further use or to whom else they may be shown;

(d) to the effect that failure to comply with any direction given under paragraph (c) may be a contempt of court;

(e) for the determination of the issue of severe financial hardship.

(5) Directions under paragraph (4) will be given on paper without a hearing unless the judge directs otherwise."

Both parties have to file a statement of assets as the hardship caused to the non-protected party – having to pay its own costs in any event – must be taken in to account when considering making the order.

The draft Civil Procedure Rules and the whole proposed scheme is of Byzantine complexity.

**Further extension**

Speaking in July 2014 Mr Justice Ramsey, who was then the judge in charge of implementing Jackson, suggested that QOCS be extended to actions against the police. He did not make it clear which of the two scheme he proposed, that is the personal injury model or the defamation model.

Actions against the police have more in common with personal injury cases than with defamation cases.

At paragraph 41 of its <u>consultation paper in relation to extending QOCS to defamation and privacy matters</u> the government states:-

"The Government is not seeking views on a further extension of costs protection to other categories of litigation at this stage, but would welcome any comments on the drafting of the rules, and whether they could be simplified or regularised in the event that it is extended further in future."

That is inherently contradictory but the main point to note is that the government clearly is considering extending the concept to other categories of litigation.

# Part V

# SET-OFF

# Chapter 13

## Set-Off

# SET OFF

The common law concept of legal set-off has existed since at least as early as 1745 – see *Hanak v Green,* Court of Appeal 1958, 2 QB 9

The Civil Procedure Rules deal with it in the briefest of terms:-

"Set-off

44.12

    (1)  Where a party entitled to costs is also liable to pay costs, the court may assess the costs which that party is liable to pay and either –

        (a)  set off the amount assessed against the amount the party is entitled to be paid and direct that party to pay any balance; or

        (b)  delay the issue of a certificate for the costs to which the party is entitled until the party has paid the amount which that party is liable to pay."

The Practice Direction is silent as to the effect of this rule.

Significantly this rule appears immediately above the rule dealing with Qualified One Way Costs Shifting – CPR 44.13 to CPR 44.17 – also notable for its brevity.

This raises the question as to whether, in a QOCS case, even the claimant's pre Part 36 costs are at risk of being eaten in to to satisfy the unsatisfied element of a costs order in favour of a defendant when a defendant's Part 36 offer has not been beaten.

Thus the claimant is awarded £30,000 at court and an order is made in the defendant's favour for £40,000, leaving an unsatisfied balance of £10,000.

May the defendant set this off against the claimant's pre Part 36 costs?

Yes, seems to be the clear answer. That situation appears to fall fairly and squarely with CPR 44.12(1)(a).

District Judge Gill considered a fixed recoverable costs matter where the claimant was awarded £2,750.00 general damages at trial but failed to beat the defendant's Part 36 offer.

The claimant was awarded costs totalling £3,952.00 up to the date of the expiry of the Part 36 offer.

The defendant was awarded costs from the date of expiry onwards totalling £5,782.00.

During the course of the litigation two other costs orders had been made with the costs being summarily assessed in each case.

The claimant had been awarded £300.00 thus creating a total entitlement to costs of £4,252.00.

The defendant had been awarded £4,492.30 costs giving a total costs entitlement of £10,274.30.

This was a Qualified One-Way Costs Shifting case but the claimant's failure to beat the defendant's Part 36 offer meant that the protection was lost. This enables the full costs order in favour of the defendant to be enforced but only to the extent of money due to the claimant, that is generally a claimant cannot be made to write a cheque.

Here the court started, entirely correctly in my view, by setting off under CPR 44.12 the claimant's entire costs entitlement against the defendant's costs entitlement and this meant that the claimant had no entitlement to costs at all and at this stage the calculation was as follows:

| | |
|---|---|
| Costs due to defendant - | £10,274.30 |
| Less costs due to claimant - | £4,252.00 |
| Balance - | £6,022.30 |

Then the court applied CPR 44.14(1) allowing the defendant to enforce further up to the extent of the claimant's damages of £2,750.00.

Thus the picture then was:

| | |
|---|---|
| Outstanding balance - | £6,022.30 |
| Less enforcement to the extent of damages - | £2,750.00 |
| Balance outstanding to defendant - | £3,272.30 |

The court declined to allow the defendant to enforce that balance as against the claimant but ordered that the defendant be at liberty to make an application that the outstanding balance of costs be paid by the credit hire organisation – parts of the claim was for credit hire charges – by virtue of CPR 44.16(3) which refers back to CPR 44.16(2).

In my view this decision is entirely correct and the order of deductions is logical, that is that the starting point should be to set off costs due to the defendant against costs due to the claimant.

What remains unclear is as to whether the defendant can set off costs made under the Portal procedure. In my view they can.

CPR 44.15 then deals with matters where the full extent of the order may be enforced without leave of the court, and those circumstances are set out there. Again this is not the whole story as by definition a court will have needed to have made an order on one of those grounds, thus effectively triggering full costs enforcement without *further leave*.

CPR 44.16 provides exceptions whereby the full order may be enforced, over and above the damages awarded, but now only with specific permission of the court.

**Case Law**

In <u>Kai Surrey v Barnet and Chase Farm Hospitals NHS Trust [2015] EWHC B 16 (Costs)</u>

the Senior Courts Costs Office considered set-off of post Part 36 costs, where a defendant's offer was not beaten, and pre-Part 36 legal aid costs.

One of the arguments was that a claimant was better off with a Conditional Fee Agreement with ATE insurance as compared with legal aid as ATE insurance would cover post Part 36 adverse costs whereas legal aid does not.

That begged the question as to whether set-off of post Part 36 costs would be against damages or pre-Part 36 costs. The answer appears to be either. In paragraphs 38 to 40 the court said:-

"38.     Mr Hutton challenged this assertion on the basis that it was more likely to be the claimant's costs that would be affected than his damages. This would occur by way of a set off between the claimant and defendant's orders for costs. Mr Hutton cited Scott LJ in the case of Lockley v National Blood Transfusion Service [1992] 1 WLR 492 where he stated:

"In general, in my opinion, interlocutory costs incurred in the progress of an action to trial and ordered to be paid by a plaintiff to a defendant would in equity impeach the right of the plaintiff to recover from the defendant costs of the action ordered to be paid by the defendant. A set-off of costs against costs, when all are incurred in the prosecution or defence of the same action, seems so natural and equitable as not to need any special justification. I would expect a party objecting to the set-off to give some special reason for the objection. It is, in my opinion, less obvious that a set-off of costs against damages would always be justified."

39.     Mr Hutton also referred to the case of R (Burkett) v London Borough of Hammersmith and Fulham [2004] EWCA Civ 1342. There, the Court of Appeal dismissed the argument run on behalf of the claimant's solicitors (and other solicitors generally) that a set off unfairly impacted on the lawyers. The Court decided that the difference between the fees calculated at between the parties' rates and at legal aid rates was a matter which must have been considered by Parliament when setting up the scheme. The fact that a set off impacted on the lawyers rather than the claimant did not prevent such an order being made.

40.     Mr Innes raised two arguments in response to the suggestion that a failure to beat a Part 36 offer only affected the claimant's lawyers. First, the question of a set off has no impact on the costs payable by the claimant under the statutory charge. Secondly, Mr Innes did not accept that costs were always set off against costs rather than damages in any event. He referred me to several paragraphs in Burkett

(quoting Scott LJ in Lockley) to show that the court had in mind the concept of costs being offset against either damages or costs depending upon the circumstances. The following is one of the propositions put forward by Scott LJ in this context:

"Set-off of costs or damages to which one party is entitled against costs or damages to which another party is entitled depends upon the application of the equitable criterion I have endeavoured to express. It was treated by May J in Currie & Co v Law Society [1977] QB 990, 1000, as a 'question for the court's discretion'. It is possible to regard all questions regarding costs as being subject to the statutory discretion conferred on the court by s51 of the [Senior Courts] Act 1981. But I would not have thought that a set-off of damages against damages could properly be described as a discretionary matter, nor that a set-off of costs against damages could be so described.'"

At paragraph 77 Master Rowley said:-

"77.     I tend to agree with the defendant's submissions in respect of set-off i.e. that it is usually against costs rather than damages, but it cannot be said in any case that it will be one rather than the other."

The logic of this must apply to Qualified One-Way Costs Shifting cases and thus where a claimant fails to beat a defendant's Part 36 offer the defendant is entitled to set-off its post Part 36 costs against the claimant's pre-Part 36 costs rather than damages. Indeed the tenor of this case and the cases that it considers suggests that the starting point is that post Part 36 costs should be set-off against costs and not damages.


In *Hanak v Green, Court of Appeal 1958, 2 QB 9*

the claimant sued the defendant in relation to defective work in the building of a property but the defendant successfully argued that a greater sum was due to him in relation to unpaid bills for work done, leaving a small balance in his favour, namely £10 1s 9d (£10.09).

The issue was as to costs. The Court of Appeal ordered the claimant to pay the defendant's costs of the main action on Scale 4 (for claims over £100) and to pay the defendant's costs on Scale 2 on his counterclaim.

This overturned the decision of the court at first instance which had awarded the claimant the costs of her claim on Scale 3 and the defendant the costs of his counterclaim/set-off on Scale 3.

The Scales at the time were:

| Sum of money | Scale |
| --- | --- |
| Exceeding £2 but not £10 | 1 |
| Exceeding £10 but not £30 | 2 |
| Exceeding £30 but not £100 | 4 |
| Exceeding £100 | 5 |

This case had the ingredients often found in building disputes. The court referred to "the conduct of a loutish workman of the defendant" and the plaintiff "who was of an excitable nature, so conducted herself in the course of the trial that she had to be committed to prison for contempt of court".

In *UWUG Ltd and Haiss v Ball* [2015] EWHC 74 (IPEC) the defendant was ordered to pay damages of £2,859.20 but had failed to beat several Part 36 offers made by the defendant whose costs far exceeded that sum.

The costs were set off against the damages and the claimant was ordered to pay the balance to the defendant.

In *Vava and others v Anglo American South Africa Limited* [2013] EWHC 2326 QB

the Queen's Bench Division of the High Court upheld an agreement between the parties whereby the claimant's solicitors agreed not to take out a recoverable After-the-Event insurance premium in return for the defendant agreeing not to enforce costs; in other words this was a form of contractual one way costs shifting.

Consequently the court refused to allow the defendant to set-off costs against an earlier order made in favour of the claimant.

Although there is discussion of whether a set-off involves "enforcing" an order for costs, that was not the basis on which the court made its decision; rather it applied the court's inherent jurisdiction "to do what is fair". (Paragraph 16).

On the particular facts of this case the court found that it would not be fair to allow the defendant to set-off the costs order in its favour against the costs order in the claimant's favour.

This decision is unlikely to be of assistance under the statutory form of Qualified One Way Costs Shifting.

In R (Burkett) v London Borough of Hammersmith and Fulham [2004] EWCA Civ 1342

the Court of Appeal considered the issue of set-off of costs within the same proceedings when the claimant was legally aided.

Here the claimant was awarded costs in the Court of Appeal and House of Lords in relation to an appeal on interlocutory matters but lost the substantive judicial review and was ordered to pay the council's costs subject to the usual legal aid restrictions, which in effect would mean that nothing would be paid to the council.

The council argued that it should be able to set-off against the amount it had to pay to the claimant the notional sum due from the claimant.

Civil legal aid has for a long time been a form of no win lower fee. Thus the legally-aided claimant's lawyers would receive the lower sum from the legal aid fund come what may in relation to the work on the failed substantive action.

However they would receive ordinary, very much higher, commercial rates for the work where they had won, those higher rates being paid by the unsuccessful council.

If set-off was allowed then the council would not have to pay that money over – it would be set-off against the notional sum due, but not payable by, the claimant. Thus the losers would be the claimant's lawyers who would receive only legal aid rates for all work done, including the work in relation to the successful part of the claim.

It was said throughout the case that the legal aid fund had no interest in the case, but presumably that is not right as if the court allowed set-off then it prevented the legal aid fund recovering that low element payable by it in any event.

The Court of Appeal allowed the set-off.

The case contains a detailed examination of the history and case law in relation to set-off.

It may be thought that this is closely analogous to the situation in Qualified One Way Costs Shifting and Part 36, that is that costs payable by the claimant to the defendant – post Part 36 costs – may be set-off against costs due from the defendant to the claimant – pre Part 36 costs. In each case the loser is the claimant's lawyer, not the claimant.

In each case the claimant's lawyer has taken on the risk and is receiving a much lower fee in the case of legal aid, but a fee nevertheless win or lose, whereas with a conditional fee agreement the lawyer risks getting nothing in the event of defeat.

It is clear from the case law that the lawyer acting under a conditional fee agreement risks getting nothing in the event of a win, where there is a failure to beat a Part 36 offer.

Nothing in the Civil Procedure Rules changes this.

"......a set-off does not place the person against whom it is asserted under any obligation to pay, but merely reduces the amount that he can recover. We do not agree that this approach is artificial, or contrary to the spirit of costs protection. The latter is not an absolute right, but something carefully moderated by specific statutory provision to which the judges in the cases just cited made careful reference. If there is any artificiality, it is for this principle to be introduced into a case where it is not the assisted party but her lawyers who are seeing to resist the set-off". (Paragraph 50).

The Court of Appeal here quoted, with approval, from *Lockley:*

"A set-off of costs against costs, where all are incurred in the prosecution and defence of the same action, seems so natural and equitable as not to need any special justification". (Paragraph 56).

These statements, and similar ones, were made in the context of legally-aided parties; it is very difficult to see why any different principle should apply to those with the benefit, if that be the right term, of Qualified One Way Costs Shifting.

In *Lockley v National Blood Transfusion Service* [1991], The Times, 11 November 1991

the Court of Appeal held that where one party was legally aided a court had jurisdiction at the interlocutory stage of proceedings to make an order for costs in favour of the other party directing that those costs be set off against either any damages or costs to which the legally aided party had or could in future become entitled in the action.

The court held that the Legal Aid Act 1988 and regulations made thereunder did not create any new right of set-off but simply preserved the rights of set-off that the general law would allow and protected them against the charge in favour of the Legal Aid Board created by section 16(6) of the Act.

The net effect was that whatever rights of set-off were available under the general law were available against legally aided parties notwithstanding the board's change.

The operation of a set-off did not place the person whose chose in action was thereby reduced or extinguished under an obligation to pay. The operation of a set-off in respect of the liability of a legally assisted person under an order for costs did not require the legally aided person to pay anything.

It did not lead to any costs being recoverable against the legally aided person and therefore nothing in the Legal Aid Act or regulations prevented set-off.

An assessment of the amount that it would be reasonable for the legally aided person to pay, as required by section 17 of the Act and Regulation 124 of the Civil Legal Aid (General) Regulation (SI 1989 No 339) did not come into play. They had nothing to do with set-off and were not a pre-condition of set-off.

Interlocutory costs incurred in the progress of an action to trial and ordered to be paid by a plaintiff to a defendant would in equity impeach the right of the plaintiff to recover from the defendant the costs of the action ordered to be paid by the defendant.

Although this case dealt with the liability of a legally aided person, rather than a "beneficiary" of Qualified One Way Costs Shifting, and although it dealt with interlocutory costs rather than the costs post Part 36, the principles are very similar indeed, that is that a financially protected person will not have physically to pay anything, but is not protected from diminution of the award by set-off of costs against that award.

Pre Part 36 costs, like all costs, belong of course to the client, not the solicitor.

Regulation 124 of the Civil Legal Aid (General) Regulations (SI 1989 No 339) provides:

"(1)    Where proceedings have been concluded in which an assisted
        person….is liable…..for costs…..no costs……shall be recoverable
        from him until the court has determined the amount of his liability in
        accordance with section 17(1)….

"(3)    The amount of an assisted person's liability for costs shall be
        determined by the court which tried or heard the proceedings".

Section 17 of the Legal Aid Act 1988 provides:

"(1)    The liability of a legally aided party under an order for costs made
        against him with respect to any proceedings shall not exceed the
        amount (if any) which is a reasonable one for him to pay having
        regard to all the circumstances, including the financial resources of all
        the parties and their conduct in connection with the dispute".

In *Wagenaar v Weekend Travel Limitedt/ a Ski Weekend and Serradji (Third Party)*
[2014] EWCA Civ 1105 (31 July 2014)

the Court of Appeal considered various aspects of Qualified One Way Costs
Shifting and at paragraph 44 said:-

"I did not gain much assistance from the cases that the parties cited that were
decided under the Legal Aid Act 1974, where there was a limited right to
enforcement of costs orders against legally aided parties. That was a quite
different statutory regime…"

However *Wagenaar* was not concerned with set-off but rather enforcement
where there was nothing to set-off. There is nothing in the *Wagenaar* decision
that suggests that the set-off cases in the context of legal aid, dealt with above,
cannot be taken in to account when the issue of set-off in a QOCS case
comes before the court.

In *Reid v Cupper* [1915] 2 KB 147

there were two actions and judgment for the Plaintiff was given in one and
judgment for the Defendant in the other. It is a helpful guide to the common
law principles of set-off.

Could the Plaintiff set off costs ordered in his favour in case he won against
costs he had to pay in the case that he lost?  Yes, notwithstanding the decision
in *David v Rees* [1904] 2 KB 435 that Order LXV, r 14, does not allow the set
off of costs in separate proceedings, the case of *Edwards v Hope* (1885) 14
QBD 922 showed that the court had a discretion to allow the set-off by the

practice previous to Reg.Hill.Terry 1852, r 63, and that the set-off was rightly ordered in the exercise of the judge's discretion. Thus the pre-1832 common law equitable jurisdiction remained in force.

## Reid v Cupper

"Before the year 1832 – speaking of the common law jurisdiction to the exclusion of that of the Court of Chancery – there was recognized what was called an equitable jurisdiction (that is to say, a jurisdiction to do that which was fair) to order a set-off. It is described by Brett M.R. in Edwards v Hope thus: "The Courts always had an equitable jurisdiction, for the purpose of preventing absurdity or injustice in cases where there had been judgments for damages between the same parties in distinct actions, to set off one judgment against the other and to allow execution to issue in respect of the balance only". Mr Matthews has cited cases which show that this was not confined to cases of judgments for damages, but extended to judgments for costs. There always was this so-called "equitable jurisdiction" to set off one judgment against the other, and execution issued only for the balance. It seems to have been done in this way: where there had been a judgment pronounced in the first action and also in the second action, the judgment in the first action could be brought before the Court on affidavit to prove that it had not been satisfied, and thereupon the Court exercised the so-called equitable jurisdiction to set off the one against the other.

That being the law before 1832, in 1832 there were passed the Reg. Gen. Hilary Term 2 Will. 4, of which r. 93, is in these words: "No set-off of damages or costs between parties shall be allowed to the prejudice of the attorney's lien for costs in the particular suit against which the set-off is sought; provided nevertheless that interlocutory costs in the same suit, awarded to the adverse party, may be deducted". The fact that "the particular suit" is mentioned there shows that there was in contemplation some other suit or action. In 1853 the rules of that year were passed, and r. 93 was reproduced in identical terms. That state of things continued until the Judicature Act 1873, came into force. Order LXV., r. 14, then provided exactly the contrary of that which had been the previous rule. The previous rule said that there should be no set-off allowed; this rule says that a set-off may be allowed. This rule is in these terms: "A set-off for damages or costs between parties may be allowed notwithstanding the solicitor's lien for costs in the particular cause or matter in which the set-off is sought". Upon that rule there has arisen a contest as to whether or not it applies to a case in which it is sought to set off costs in two independent actions".

In *Federal Commerce Ltd v Molena Alpha Inc,* C A [1978] 1 QB

the court said:

"But the courts of equity, as was their wont, came in to mitigate the technicalities of the common law. They allowed deductions – by way of equitable set off – whenever there were good equitable grounds for directly impeaching the demand which the credit was seeking to enforce: see *Rawson v Samuel* (1841) CR. & Ph. 161, 178-179, *per* Lord Cottenham L C. These grounds were never precisely formulated before the Judicature Act 1873. It is now far too late to search through the old books and dig them out. Over 100 years have passed since the Judicature Act 1873. During that time the streams of common law and equity have flown together and combined so as to be indistinguishable the one from the other. We have no longer to ask ourselves: what would the courts of common law or the courts of equity have done before the Judicature Act? We have to ask ourselves: what should we do now so as to ensure fair dealing between the parties? See *United Scientific Holdings Ltd v Burnley Borough Council* [1978] A C 904 per Lord Diplock. This question must be asked in each case as it arises for decision: and then, from case to case, we shall build up a series of precedents to guide those who come after us. But one thing is quite clear: it is not every cross-claim which can be deducted. It is only cross-claims that arise out of the same transaction or are closely connected with it. And it is only cross-claims which go directly to impeach the plaintiff's demands, that is, so closely connected with his demands that it would be manifestly unjust to allow him to enforce payment without taking into account the cross-claim. Such was the case with the lost vehicle in *Morgan & Son Ltd v S Martin Johnson & Co Ltd* [1949] 1 K B 107 and the widow's misconduct in *Hanak v Green*, Court of Appeal 1958, 2 QB 9."

This is a separate power from that of a taxing master, or costs judge, to set-off costs orders either within the same proceedings or in separate proceedings.

"It would be a serious proposition if, however much a solicitor had multiplied his costs, the Court were powerless to prevent him from getting out of the adverse party the costs due from his own client which their client may not be able to pay" (*Reid v Cupper*, Pickford L J).

This followed *Edwards v Hope* (1885) 14 QBD 922 in which the Court of Appeal held that it had power, upon an application to set-off cross judgments in distinct actions, to order that the set-off shall be subject to the lien for costs of the solicitor of the opposite party, for, assuming that rule 14 applies to a set-off in distinct actions, it leaves the court a discretion to allow the set-off, either subject to or notwithstanding the solicitor's lien. This followed the repeal of Reg.Hil.Term, 1853, r. 63 which had provided.

"No set-off of damages or costs between parties shall be allowed to the prejudice of the attorney's lien for costs in the particular suit against which the set-off is sought.......provided nevertheless, that interlocutory costs in the same suit, awarded to the adverse party, may be deducted".

The courts had recognised the injustice of allowing a solicitor's lien to prevail when the opposite party had substantially succeeded and recognised that at common law a debt or damages in one action may be set off against costs in another action.

Many of these issues stemmed from the fact that counterclaims were only introduced by the Supreme Court of Judicature Act 1873 and thus prior to that disputes between the same parties were subject to separate claims.

"The courts, however, always had an equitable jurisdiction, for the purpose of preventing absurdity or injustice in cases where there had been judgments for damages between the same parties in distinct actions, to set-off one judgment against the other and to allow execution to issue in respect of the balance only". (*Edwards v Hope*).

The courts retained, and always had had, a discretion "to set off against each other cross judgments in the same action or in different actions and in the same or in different courts".

Incidentally the indemnity principle does not seem to have been treated with the importance that late C20 and C21st lawyers treat it. "It appears from the judgment of James, L J, in ex parte Griffin, In re Adams 14 Ch D 37, that Lord Eldon, in *Hall v Ody* 2 B and P 28, expressed his surprise at finding that it was the practice of the Court of Common Pleas that the attorney should not take his costs out of the fund which by his diligence he recovered for his client where the opposite party was entitled to a set off."

In *re A Bankruptcy Notice* [No 171 of 1934] Court of Appeal 23 March 1934, the Court of Appeal said:

"With regard to the word "set-off", that is a word well known and established in its meaning; it is something which provides a defence because the nature and quality of the sum so relied upon are such that it is a sum which is proper to be dealt with as diminishing the claim which is made, and against which the sum so demanded can be set off".

In *National Westminster Bank plc v Skelton* [1993] 1 WLR 72

The judge stated

"…the court might consider that it would be unjust to allow the bank to enforce payment against the company without taking into account the cross-claim – in other words, that it might allow a set-off." (paragraph 247).

"But it is a special and privileged type of cross-claim, because its effect is to extinguish the original claim and prevent its establishment, rather than merely to provide a sum to be balanced off against the claim once established. That is why the rule in relation to this type of set-off is that it must "impeach" the plaintiff's demand: see the exposition of Lord Denning MR in *Federal Commerce & Navigation Co Ltd v Molena Alpha Inc [1978]*."

Set-off is set to take-off with the storm of Qualified One Way Costs Shifting which is about to break over us.

# Part VI

# REFERENCES

# Chapter 14

# References

# REFERENCES AND SOURCES

## Statutes

Administration of Justice Act 1985, s 29

Assize of Clarendon 1166

Assize of Northampton 1176

Attorneys in County Courts Act 1235

Civil Liability and Courts Act 2004 (Republic of Ireland)

County Courts Act 1984 s 52

Courts and Legal Services Act 1990 s 58(2), s 58(4)

Crime and Courts Act 2013

Criminal Injuries Compensation Act 1995, s 11(1)

Criminal Justice and Courts Act 2015, s 57

Defamation Act 1996

Distress Act 1267

Fatal Accidents Act 1976

Fatal Accidents Act and Law Reform (Miscellaneous Provisions) Act 1934

Income and Corporation Taxes Act 1988 s 148

Income Tax (Earnings and Pensions) Act 2003 s 406

Judicature Act 1873

Law Reform (Miscellaneous Provisions) Act 1934 s 1(1)

Legal Aid Act 1949

Legal Aid Act 1974

Legal Aid Act 1988

Legal Aid, Sentencing and Punishment of Offenders Act 2012

Limitation Act 1623

Lord Denman's Act 1840

Poor Persons Act 1495

Recovery of Damages and Costs Act 1278

Senior Courts Act 1981 s 33

Slander of Women Act 1891

Statute of Elizabeth c.6

Statute of Gloucester 1277

Statute of Marlbridge 1267

Statute of Westminster 1275

Supreme Court of Judicature Act 1873

1531 Statute (Henry VIII c.15)

1606 Statute of 4 James I c.3

**Statutory Instruments**

Civil Legal Aid (General) Regulations (SI 1989 No. 339)

Civil Procedure Rules 1998 (SI 1998 No. 3132)

Civil Procedure (Amendment) Rules 2013

Criminal Justice and Courts 2015 (Commencement No. 1, Saving and Transitional Provisions) Order 2015 (SI 2015 No. 778)

## Civil Procedure Rules

CPR 2.3 (1)

CPR 3.19 (5) (b)

CPR 27.14 (2) (g)

CPR 36

CPR 43.2 (1) (k) (i-iii)

CPR 44.12

CPR 44.13 to CPR 44.17

CPR 44.13 (1)

CPR 44.13 (1) (k) (i-iii)

CPR 44.15 (a)

CPR 48.2

CPR 48.2 (1)

CPR 48.2 (1) (aa)

CPR 48.2 (1) (bb)

CPR 48.2(1) (a) (i)

CPR 48.2 (1) (a) (i) (aa)

CPR 52.9 (A)

CPR 52.9 (A) (4)

**Practice Directions**

Practice Direction 44, section II

**Case Law**

AB v CD [2011] EWHC 602 (Ch)

Ahern v Bus Éireann [2011] IESC 44

Akhtar and Khan v Ball, Walsall County Court, Unreported, 10 July 2015

Alpha Rocks Solicitors v Alade [2015] EWCA Civ 685

Bee v Jenson [2007] EWCA Civ 923

Behan v Allied Irish Banks Plc [2009] IEHC 554

Birmingham City Council v Jaddoo UKEAT/0448/04/LA

*Black v Arriva North East Limited* [2014] EWCA Civ 1115

Boland v Dublin CityCouncil and Others [2011] 1EHC 176

*Brahilika v Allianz Insurance plc*, unreported, 30 July 2015

*Brian Kite v Phoenix Pub Grou*p 2015 Unreported

Carmello v Casey and another

Casseldine v The Diocese of Llandaff Board for Social Responsibly (a charity) 3 July 2015

*Clutterbuck and others v HSBC plc and others*, Chancery Division, 2 October 2015

*Chawla v Hewlett Packard Ltd* [2015] IRLR 356 EAT

*Creech v Severn Valley Railway*, 25 March 2015, Telford County Court, Unreported

*Currie & Co v Law Society* [1977] QB 990

Da' Bell v NSPCC [2010] IRLR 19 EAT

*David v Rees* [1904] 2 KB 435

Davison v Leitch [2013] EWHC 3092 (QB)

Dar Al Arkan Real Estate Company v Al Refai [2015] EWHC 1793 (Comm)

*Day v Day* [2006] EWCA Civ 415

*Dietz v Lennig Chemicals* [1969] 1 AC 170

Dunleavy v Swan Park Ltd. [2011] IEHC 232

Edwards v Hope (1885) 14 QBD 922

Excalibur Ventures LLC v Texas Keystone Inc & Ors [2014] EWHC 3436 (Comm)

Farrell v Dublin Bus [2010]1EHC 327

Federal Commerce Ltd v Molena Alpha Inc, C A [1978] 1 QB

*Flatman and Germany v Weddall and Barchester Health Care Limited* [2013] EWCA Civ 278

Folan v Mairtin Corraion and others [2011] IEHC 487

*Gilbert v Endean* [1878] 9 Ch D 259

*Gosling v Screwfix and Another, Cambridge County Court*, 29 March 2014, unreported

*Hanak v Green*, Court of Appeal 1958, 2 QB 9

Hayward v Zurich Insurance Company plc [2015] EWCA Civ 327 under appeal to Supreme Court-UKSC 2015/0099

Higgins v Caldark Ltd

*HM Prison Service v Salmon* [2001] IRLR 425

*JE v Secretary of State for the Home Department* [2014] EWCA Civ 192

*Landau v The Big Bus Company*, 31 October 2014, Master Haworth SCCO

*Leung v Eftekhari and Eftekhari* [2015] Central London County Court, 20 October 2015

*Lockley v National Blood Transfusion Service* [1991], The Times, 11 November 1991

*LSC v F, A and V* [2011] EWHC 899 (QB)

Ludlow v Unsworth and Zurich Insurance [2013] IEHC 153

*Medcalf v Mardell* [2002] 3 WLR 172

*Masood v Zahoor (Practice Note)* [2009] EWCA Civ 650

Meehan v BKNS Curtain Walling Systems Ltd and others [2012] IEHC 441

*Morgan & Son Ltd v S Martin Johnson & Co Ltd* [1949] 1 K B 107

*Moorthy v Commissioners for HM Revenue and Customs* [2015] IRLR 4 UKFTT

*Multiplex Constructions UK Ltd v Cleveland Bridge UK Ltd* [2008] EWHC 2280 TCC

*National Westminster Bank plc v Skelton* [1993] 1 WLR 72

Nolan v Kerry Foods Ltd. [2012] IEHC 208

Nolan v Mitchell and another [2012] IEHC 151

*Orthet Ltd v Vince-Cain* [2004] IRLR 857 EAT

*Ozog v Cadogan Hotel Partners Ltd* [2014] EqLR 691 EAT

*Pereira de Souza v Vinci Construction UK Ltd* UK EAT/0328/14

*R (Burkett) v London Borough of Hammersmith and Fulham* [2004] EWCA Civ 1342

*R (Corner House Research) v Secretary of State for Trade and Industry* [2005] EWCA Civ 192

*Rawson v Samuel* (1841) CR. & Ph. 161

*re A Bankruptcy Notice* [No 171 of 1934]

*Reid v Cupper* [1915] 2 KB 147

Salako v O'Carroll [2013]1EHC 17

*Samantha Woodward v Cardiff Council, Cardiff County Court, 19 August 2015*

*Sibthorpe and Morris v Southwark London Borough Council (Law Society intervening)* [2011] EWCA Civ 25.

Simmons v Castle (2012) EWCA 1039

*The Sash Window Workshop Ltd v King* [2015] IRLR 348 EAT

*Solland v Clifford Harris and Co [2015] EWHC 3259 (Ch)*

*Summers v Fairclough Homes Ltd* [2012] UKSC 26

*Thinc Group Ltd v Jeremy Kingdom* [2013] EWCA Civ 1306

*Timothy James Consulting Ltd v Wilton* [2015] IRLR 368 EAT

*United Scientific Holdings Ltd v Burnley Borough Council* [1978] A C 904

*UWUG Ltd and Haiss v Ball* [2015] EWHC 74 (IPEC)

*Vava and others v Anglo American South Africa Limited* [2013] EWHC 2326 QB

*Vento v Chief Constable of West Yorkshire Police (No 2)* [2002] IRLR 102 Court of Appeal

Waliszewski v McArthur and Company(Steel and Metal Ltd), High Court of Ireland,24 April 2015 Unreported

Wall v British Canoe Union, Birmingham County Court 30 July 2015

*Wagenaar v Weekend Travel Limitedt/ a Ski Weekend and Serradji (Third Party)*
[2014] EWCA Civ 1105

*Webb v Liverpool Womens' NHS Foundation Trust* [2015] EWHC 449 (QB)


**Other**


Criminal Injuries Compensation Scheme 2012

Employment Tribunals: Presidential Guidance

Frederick, Sir Pollock and Frederic William Maitland: The History of English Law before the Time of Edward I

Hansard: House of Commons, 25 November 2015

Hansard: House of Lords, 23 July 2014

Jackson, Lord Justice: Preliminary Report

Jackson, Lord Justice: Final Report

Law Society Gazette: 5 September 2015

Motor Insurers' Bureau: Uninsured Driver's Agreement

Motor Insurers' Bureau: Untraced Driver's Agreement

Oxford English Dictionary

Roget's Thesaurus

Shorter Oxford English Dictionary

Statement to Parliament: Chancellor of the Exchequer 25 November 2015

Sutherland, Donald W. The Assize of Novel Disseisin :Oxford University Press 21 June 1973

Underwood, Kerry: Personal Injury Revolutionised: Criminal Justice and Courts Act 2015